THOUGHT LEADERSHIP

THOUGHT LEADERSHIP

Moving Hearts and Minds

Robin Ryde

First published 2007 by
PALGRAVE MACMILLAN
Houndmills, Basingstoke, Hampshire RG21 6XS and
175 Fifth Avenue, New York, N. Y. 10010
Companies and representatives throughout the world

PALGRAVE MACMILLAN is the global academic imprint of the Palgrave Macmillan division of St. Martin's Press, LLC and of Palgrave Macmillan Ltd. Macmillan® is a registered trademark in the United States, United Kingdom and other countries. Palgrave is a registered trademark in the European Union and other countries.

ISBN-13: 978-0-230-52551-1
ISBN-10: 0-230-52551-2

This book is printed on paper suitable for recycling and made from fully managed and sustained forest sources. Logging, pulping and manufacturing processes are expected to conform to the environmental regulations of the country of origin.

A catalogue record for this book is available from the British Library.

A catalog record for this book is available from the Library of Congress.

10   9   8   7   6   5   4   3   2   1
16   15   14   13   12   11   10   09   08   07

Printed and bound in Great Britain by
Creative Print & Design (Wales), Ebbw Vale

This book is dedicated to Jackson and his grandparents

I would like to thank Sue Duncan for keeping me on the straight and narrow and leaving me with no excuses to give up writing this book. With special thanks to Lisa, who has brought inspiration, support, and profound questions that have often stopped me in my tracks. This book is considerably better for it. Thanks.

Additional thanks go to the following people who have shaped, supported and made an invaluable contribution to this book (they may not know it but they have): Henry Broughton, Chuck Dymer, Rob Fisher, Steve Mcguirk, Cathy Preece, Rob Reynolds, Chris Rodgers, Kath Way, and all the participants of the Top Management Programme

Contents

List of Tables

Introduction

Leadership and organizational change starts with thinking. Thinking about problems, thinking about possibilities, and thinking about capabilities.

But thinking never occurs in a vacuum. Long gone are the days when a chief executive officer would disappear for weeks with a towel over his head only to reappear to announce 'the answer' to the organization. Thinking is of course a social activity that sees people coming together to develop and share ideas. People are authors of the world they live in and not passive recipients.

Conversations are the forums within which thinking is developed. They are the crucible within which ideas are made and adopted. The job of leadership is to use the process of social thinking to produce excellent ideas and to bring about change where needed.

Anyone interested in change or leadership needs to understand what is going on in the thinking process. Why, for example, meetings rarely achieve what they set out to. Why thinking conversations have a horrible sense of déjà vu. Why sometimes when people come together great things happen and on other occasions it seems like a shocking waste of time, money, and energy. Why discussions about change always seem to end in resistance and worry.

To shift the way people think and feel is easy. But it requires an understanding of how thinking habits draw discussions along unseen channels. It requires an understanding of the trajectory that different thinking habits follow. And above all it requires leaders at every level to become masters of the social thinking process. Conversation and what we say to one another is the basis of all leadership and change. This book provides a blueprint of how we can move hearts and minds and create incredible results along the way.

Two Ways to Read This Book

This book has been written so that it can be read in two ways:

- The 'scenic route' – Chapters 1, 2, and 3. For the serious reader who would enjoy a wider appreciation of the issues and the opportunity to engage with a variety of illustrations and real life examples

- The 'shortcut' – Chapters 1 and 3. For the practically minded reader who wants to learn quickly how to lead thinking and bring about change more effectively

1 Thinking on Autopilot

Like raindrops on a windowpane

Whether we are talking about decisions in the boardroom or conversation at the dinner table, the way in which we think about challenges and problems is surprisingly similar regardless of the test that we face. We witness this every day although we may not fully register what is happening. It is perhaps easiest to picture what is going on as a raindrop winding its way down a windowpane. The raindrop represents the movement and direction of our thinking once a problem or conversation is explored. In every sense, the raindrop could take almost any route down the window were it not for two important factors. The first is gravity, which puts pressure on the raindrop to take the most direct route, and the second is the path already taken by previous raindrops, which act as channels encouraging subsequent raindrops to follow the same route. Our thinking is the same. We have a limited range of thinking styles that we are pulled towards with almost gravitational force, and we find ourselves stuck in the channels of thinking already created, either by others in the course of conversation or through our own habits. One consequence is that we have a limited repertoire of thinking styles that possess great problem-solving power, but on their own are entirely inadequate. Another is that if we wish to shift the way people think and to lead change we need to work at the roots of the thinking process – the unseen channels that shape our interactions.

For quite some years, I have been running leadership development programs for well-established senior figures and for younger, highflyers who are identified as likely to travel to the top of their organizations. These have been some of the largest leadership development investments in Europe, engaging people from all sectors. I have, over the years, had the privilege of working with some of the most impressive people around – whether as participants on my programs or the scores of Chief Executive Officers, Chairs, or members of a Board that I have engaged with as part of the program. During this time, I have provided a curriculum, for want of a better word, around the topic of leadership; a subject that still fascinates me after all these years. In addition to setting the agenda in terms of development, I have also been able to observe the interaction of people when they have come together to solve problems, to learn from each other, and, at times, to review their life decisions.

An important component of the programs I've led are the numerous occasions when the groups have undertaken live case study examinations of other organizations across the public and private sector. These have usually taken the form of intensive visits to case study organizations, usually focusing on a particular set of issues and involving interviews with staff at every level. In each case time is often spent with customers and clients, stakeholders, the top team, the change agents, and at the front line. The deliverable for these exercises has always been a formal presentation to the sponsoring Chief Executive Officer and usually his or her top team. The requirement for the program participants is to add value to leadership group thinking and ultimately, to influence that group to take action. This is always a tough task, not least because time may be limited to two or three days and the program participants start with more or less zero knowledge of the organization studied.

Setting aside the content of these case studies, there is a great deal of learning that can be derived from the processes adopted by people as they work in groups. Often participants sadly miss the learning about process, instead becoming embroiled in the task. This is not at all unusual, particularly among senior people who have often got to where they are in their organizations through being excellent problem solvers, and not necessarily through being reflective individuals. For me, though, I have had an invaluable opportunity to stand back a little and observe what is going on and to look across different programs and see if patterns emerge in terms of process.

Going back to our live case studies, I have observed two very dominant patterns in the way people come together to explore issues. The first is that as people begin to gather data on a topic, they very quickly start to search for deficiencies in what they see. For example, if in a meeting or through written documentation participants identified the central vision or strategy for an organization, they would then hunt down instances in which that vision or strategy was not being followed. So if an organization had the explicit intention, let's say, to help the homeless, people would try to challenge and test that intention perhaps by questioning whether it meant all homeless people; or what would happen if some homeless people didn't want to be helped; or why wasn't this being done by the government?

A different example is a case study I undertook with a globally renowned company that is well known for its creativity and innovation. The group that visited the company seemed hell bent on challenging whether the company was, in fact, creative at all. For each and every person that was interviewed, participants on the program would report 'well Mr A wasn't at all wacky; he was just like you or me'. Or it would be 'they can talk a good game but I'm just not convinced'.

Another illustration of this behavior is when, on a separate occasion, a very successful and high profile entrepreneur in the media industry was brought in to give a keynote presentation that very well demonstrated the merits of an entrepreneurial approach to business. The group on this occasion represented larger companies and organizations that, in most cases, had existed for at least a handful of decades. There was a mixture of positive and negative murmuring during the presentation until at the end one of the participants quite pointedly asked 'why are you here and what do you expect us to learn from you?' Quite apart from the tone that this conveyed, the question that was put was a deficit-focused question. It was intended to find fault and the implication could only have been that the speaker had not, at least for the individual asking the question, convinced them of their view.

The important point that I want to make using these illustrations is that this style of thinking and questioning, whether it is to find deficiencies in an organization's strategy or to be eternally skeptical about other people's views is a completely 'normal' and routine way of thinking about the world and about business. In my line of business I would, at the drop of a hat, replace deficit-based questioning, for learning-based inquiry, so that every step of the way whether listening to somebody speaking or visiting other companies, the question that people have in their minds is 'what can I learn from this?' It would perhaps be different if we were out on the African savannahs and had to quickly detect whether a movement in the long grass was a lion or a bird. In that scenario, the risk or the problem needs to be diagnosed in less than a second, but as exciting and quick-paced as business can be, we should not feel the compulsion to crush what we are looking at as if it were our enemy.

The second very dominant pattern that I see rehearsed time and time again is what I describe as a 'common sense' approach to challenges and issues. Common Sense Thinking is about applying a broad and general set of principles to a given situation so as to advance thinking on that subject. It is extraordinarily useful and, in very many situations, will deliver a sensible and helpful answer to your questions.

However common sense is, of course, a substitute for expertise and specific experience and because we don't always have that expertise to hand, we typically bridge the gap with common sense. An illustration of this is some internal consultancy I lead a few years ago to design, for the first time in the organization, a talent management program to select and develop 'high potential' staff. One of the very many questions to be answered was whether the program, once on its feet, should be low profile or whether it should be, along with the people selected and their promotion performance, openly communicated and shared across the organization – the principle being 'why hide what we are doing?' In discussions with the top team of the organization this was taken as a focus for the thinking and the view was held that, because the organization didn't want to appear underhand or elitist, the program should be visible, high profile, and communication should be bold so as not to imply any dishonesty or favoritism. On the face of it, this seemed a very sensible proposal and one that appeared to fit with the developing culture of the organization – one that was moving towards greater honesty and transparency.

Research undertaken for this work told a different story. The messages emerging from the 20 organizations benchmarked, many of which had operated talent management programs for years, were that because of the enormous sensitivity surrounding high potential programs, success was more likely to be achieved through adopting a lower profile and keeping processes transparent and honest but low key. Further research into first time programs in organizations at a similar cultural transitionary stage confirmed the case for a low profile operation.

Once again the point is not whether to have high or low profile talent management programs, rather that Common Sense Thinking can make absolute sense and, on one level, be entirely justifiable but may simply be inadequate.

Table 1.1 highlights the basic repertoire of thinking engines that we use, including Deficit Thinking and Common Sense Thinking processes. In most cases, we deploy two or three of these thinking engines, often not aware of any explicit selection that they are the most appropriate method. They seem to come naturally to us and in every sense we take them for granted. They have served us well for a long time but, because they are adopted almost by default, they may not always be the right choice. They also possess quite considerable limitations if they do not fit with the thinking required. Finally, and arguably most importantly, if we want to shape the way people think and to move people or organizations to a particular destination we need to understand these thinking habits; how they work and what

Table 1.1 Standard thinking repertoire

Standard thinking repertoire	Description
Deficit Thinking	Thinking that focuses on faults, shortcomings, and weaknesses in the target of the discussion
Rational Thinking	Thinking that accentuates the logical component to a problem or challenge. Solutions are characterized as steps in a logical sequence
Sticky Thinking	In the course of conversation, thinking is developed as one person forms an association with the last point of view raised; thoughts stick to each other and shape the thinking process
Common Sense Thinking	Common Sense Thinking is practiced where people seek to solve a problem or challenge by applying general and inexpert knowledge. A rational thinking model is often drawn upon
Binary Thinking	When solutions to challenges or problems are characterized as one thing or another; as opposing ends of a spectrum – the implication being that such options are separate and mutually exclusive
Equity Thinking	Thinking that uses the concept of fairness as its overriding principle

we can do to use them much more effectively. In the next paragraphs, I will explain each of these in a little more detail.

Deficit Thinking

I can think of an occasion, in my personal life, when Deficit Thinking almost certainly saved someone's life. I was on a SCUBA diving holiday with my partner in a remote region famed for its exquisite coral and plankton blooms. We had arrived there in the evening and the following day and everyday afterwards, we had jumped in the boat to be taken to places where the currents went in every direction and fish stood on their tails to stay still. It was beautiful and exciting, with drift dives that seemed to take us at 20 mph just a few feet from the coral walls. It was a morning dive like any other; up at 6.30 am, breakfast, on the boat to take us to the foot of an old volcano. The dive went very well, in fact so well that afterwards, as I sunned myself on the top of the deck, my partner plunged back into the water to do some impromptu snorkeling. Like me she was an addict and didn't want to waste the time it took to decompress before the afternoon dive. The boat had a skeleton crew on it because of elections that were taking place on the mainland. The boat hadn't been moored and so the captain, also our dive leader, intermittently started the engine to take us away from the coral that grew close to the surface. The boat drifted towards it every now and then and, with the help of the engine, returned to its original site.

I distinctly remember lying on my back and feeling truly relaxed. I had got over the jet lag and felt at one with the water when I heard screams from down below. Something had happened and the boat's engine made some deep rumblings. Amid even more shrill screams, I jumped off the top deck to see my partner being lifted vertically out of the water by the burly, six-feet-tall German captain. She had been hit by the boat's propeller as it had drifted into the coral and the engine had been started without warning. She looked shocked but undamaged until we took her wet suit off. The propeller hadn't touched her, but the force of the water spun by the propeller had cut through her wet suit and deep into her leg leaving a very long cut about 9 inches across, and deep enough to cut into the muscle. It was horrifying. There were other large wounds elsewhere on her legs.

We frantically called a speedboat to take us to the shore; it collected us and, as it arrived on the mainland, we found ourselves in a makeshift ambulance that trundled to the hospital, each moment costing us valuable time. We arrived at the hospital and my partner was immediately ushered onto another makeshift piece of equipment, this time an operating table. At this point we found ourselves, despite the shock and the ever-growing seriousness of the situation, demanding that we saw all the implements that were to be used. We questioned every step of the process, 'is he a trained surgeon?' 'Are those needles clean?' (They weren't, and we asked them to be changed which they did politely), 'are you sure those scalpels are clean?'(Some weren't which were also changed). The repair work conducted by the doctors was, in the event, excellent. The less than sterile nature of some of the equipment was a serious concern but we think we managed to track down all of the offending items having them replaced. My partner fully recovered although the ordeal wasn't over as we encountered numerous difficulties negotiating with airlines for them to provide sufficient seat space to take my partner home with her leg sticking out at right angles, but that's another story.

The outcome, given the circumstances, was a good one. Along the way our Deficit Thinking, for example in relentlessly looking for faults or risks in the cleanliness of the equipment used, served us extremely well and may have made the difference, particularly in light of the extreme humidity in the country, between life and death or at least serious illness.

Deficit Thinking, as illustrated by this example, is an incredibly powerful thinking mode to adopt. It is designed principally to help us detect danger, to secure our own survival. It is useful too in domestic or business settings. Every time we evaluate something we need to understand where the weaknesses lie, what too are the risks. Picking a good builder needs an eye for unreliability or untidiness. Interviewing applicants for a job needs an eye for incompetence or untrustworthiness. Listening to a sales pitch needs an ear for dishonesty or important omissions.

Not every scenario though is suitable for Deficit Thinking wherein the wider challenge lies. There is no doubt that we overuse this style of thinking. Almost every scenario that calls upon us to think somehow attracts it. One of the many complications in using the deficit model is in the impact on people when it is deployed. In working with young highflyers, particularly in more established sectors such as the legal field, engineering, audit and accountancy, banking, and administrative functions I have noticed the overuse of the Deficit Thinking model in communications. An example is where I have worked with teams within organizations to deliver their perspective to the top team, (often based on group research), of how the organization might develop and improve. This is commonly done with highflyers to encourage their engagement with corporate and strategic issues at an ever-earlier stage in their careers. In this kind of situation I have seen, in almost every occasion, groups providing to the top team, in considerable detail, a long list of problems-to-be-solved. Excellent analyses of organizational weaknesses in leadership, culture, structure, communications, policies, motivation, mission, vision, strategy, values, change programs, and more besides, and always very little in terms of solutions. The mountain that the organization needs to climb is described in fine detail. The rocks, the loose scree, the slippery mud, the thorny bushes, the potholes, the wet grass, the altitude sickness, and the stories of failures from the last party that tried to climb the mountain. The result, of course, is not only an account that provides far fewer solutions than problems but a presentation that leaves the audience and the customer exhausted and without the will to carry on. The deficit model, for all its strength, drains the life out of all of us leaving a garbage tip of woes for us to contemplate. This is particularly important in times of change when leaders often overemphasize the weaknesses found in the organization as a motivation, a rationale for change. Of course, staff that feel directly implicated in those weaknesses don't always have the same hunger or energy to change as the top team.

The deficit model, like the other basic thinking engines outlined in this chapter, has become part of our thinking habit and this is where it becomes dangerous to us. We adopt the deficit model usually without hesitation and, like a knight wielding a sword; it is used as often to kill our opponent, as it is to open letters. Sooner or later, we too become the victim of our choice of weapon and we turn it on ourselves – finding flaws in ourselves; prodding at weaknesses, exposing our own wounds, and toying with them. Many years ago I shared an office with a colleague who at the best of times was cantankerous. He had a son in his teens and it was clear from the often-short conversations he held with him over the phone that the relationship wasn't a good one. It came to a head one day when my colleague after a fairly heated telephone exchange said: 'the thing is son, you're "yesterday's man!"' They were horrible words for me to hear, but I am sure considerably more damaging to the teenager. The deficit model is so routine for us we forget how destructive it can be, and we forget too how little attention we are paying to solutions and offering help while we are demolishing the subject matter.

It is useful here to touch on the subject of habit since this is what is leading us, ironically without thinking, to adopting our thinking styles. In their book *The Social Construction of Reality*, Peter Berger and Thomas Luckmann illustrate this well:

> All human activity is subject to habitualization. Any action that is repeated frequently becomes cast into a pattern, which can be reproduced with an economy of effort ... Habitualization carries with it the important psychological gain that choices are narrowed. While in theory there may be a hundred ways to go about the project of building a canoe out of matchsticks, habitualization narrows these down to one. (p. 52)

Robert Wuthnow, elaborating on the theories of the social anthropologist Mary Douglas, extends this point a little further:

> The moral order is so infused into our structuring of reality that activities such as sorting, tidying, cleaning and putting things in their place in general act to re-enforce not only the structure of social reality but of moral sentiments too. That moral component of assigning reality to different categories becomes particularly

apparent when things get out of place. At that point we are socially obliged to reset the structure of things and thereby re-enforce the fabric of social and moral order. (p. 87)

What is argued here is that not only can our practices become habits that, by their nature, narrow our options (thus making those practices efficient), but also that our tendency to reduce, to order, and to have things in their place (in this case using a narrow range of thinking practices in conversation), carries with it a form of 'moral' force that this is the right thing to do. For people therefore in a conversational setting to introduce modes of thinking and discussion that fall outside of the tacitly accepted repertoire, invites a negative response almost as if the morals of conduct had been transgressed.

The next time you are at a meeting, quietly count the number of times the conversation turns to deficits. Observe also the impact this has on the direction of the conversation and the energy levels generated. Notice too how the deficit thinking process is entirely understood as a legitimate mode of discussion without once being referred to or called upon.

Rational Thinking

In Cincinnati there is an independent non-profit organization called the Association for Rational Thought. The organization has been around for almost 15 years and is committed to 'balanced and rational exploration of the world'. In addition to its central aim, it also encourages well-informed evaluation of fringe-science, pseudo-science and paranormal claims:

> While many of us are not scientists, we embrace the scientific method as humankind's best invention for seeking knowledge. Sceptics are not cynics. We don't simply reject every unusual idea. We do insist that unusual ideas require considerable supporting evidence before we accept them as being true.

There is a similar society run by students at Stanford University (called RATT). In their statement of philosophy they state:

> All of us agree that any belief, even society's sacred cows, is potentially up for scrutiny, and we strive to base our responses to ideas always on the available evidence. Above all, we would

like to encourage a scientific, rational outlook on life and to further skills necessary to survive in today's pseudoscientific information age.

In the divisions of IBM responsible for software development there are groups of people named as 'rational thought leaders' who debate and platform their views on the value of rational thinking in the business. The group have authored numerous books on the subject with titles ranging from *The Rational Unified Process Made Easy* to a newsletter called *The Rational Edge*.

There is even a Rationalist Press Association based in London that 'promotes reason and evidence in the understanding of life' and draws from a tradition of rational thought stretching back to the seventeenth century.

Rational thought is another of our dominant thinking habits, reaching for some, as these real life examples illustrate, an almost evangelical status in the modern world. One definition of Rationalism is 'the belief or principle that actions and opinions should be based on reason rather than on emotion or religion'[1]. The process of applying rational thinking draws upon logic as a fundamental engine and upon well established techniques such as deductive method, where hypotheses are tested against available data and evidence; and inductive method, where data is found and built from the bottom up into hypotheses and grounded theories. In the practice of rational thinking, at least in business settings, we find ourselves following some trusted approaches such as describing, comparing, spotting repeated events and patterns, looking for sequences, considering the weight of evidence, extrapolating and drawing inferences, exploring association and causality between different data, breaking down issues into their component parts, and always testing our thinking against a model of 'reasonableness'.

The use of a rational model in thinking and in interaction is clearly a powerful weapon in our armory. Without it we would be lost. But, like our Deficit Thinking approach it has become a habit and, as such, its merits and shortfalls have somehow slipped under the radar.

I am reminded of the Myers Briggs Type Inventory tool, which is widely used in business to profile individual, team and sometimes in organizational preferences. The tool is based on the work of Carl Jung who made his thoughts explicit in the book *Psychological Type* first printed in 1921. It was later developed in the 1940s by a mother and daughter team, who developed Jung's theory of psychological type into four polarities which were labeled as 'Introvert–Extrovert'; 'Intuition–Sensing'; 'Thinking–Feeling'; and 'Judging–Perceiving'.

It is estimated that more than four million people take the Myers Briggs test each year.

It is interesting in the context of the rational thinking model because it helps to illuminate the blind spots that are not always apparent to us as we unthinkingly step into rational mode. The Myers Briggs polarity of most interest here is the 'Thinking – Feeling' continuum. Those of us that have a 'Thinking' preference tend to accentuate the rational side of our thinking. We like to analyze pros and cons, and then be consistent and logical in progressing our thoughts. We like to be impersonal and to apply an objective perspective to a given situation. Those of us with a 'Feeling' preference attend more to the feelings and values of others. We are more empathetic and draw upon our own appreciation for relationships and the views people hold. Our thinking is not illogical; rather it values how people might be affected by decisions; how harmony and consensus might be achieved, and how people feel.

Those of you that have participated in any form of training that helps you deal with the media will know that the first lesson, when communicating difficult news to an audience, is to always speak to how people are feeling. In the horrific bombings in London on 7 July 2005, the Prime Minister halted the G8 summit in Scotland to speak to the country. The announcement from 10 Downing Street was:

> This is a terrible and tragic atrocity that has cost many innocent lives. I have just attended a meeting of the Government's emergency committee. I received a full report from the ministers and officials responsible. There will be an announcement made in respect of the various services; in particular we hope the Underground, as far as is possible and rail and bus services are up and running as soon as possible.
> I would like to express my profound condolences to the families of the victims and to those who are casualties of this terrorist act. I would also like to thank the emergency services that have been magnificent today in every respect. There, of course, will now be the most intense Police and Security Service action to make sure we bring those responsible to justice. I would also pay tribute to the stoicism and resilience of the people of London who have responded in a way typical of them.

The speech was exactly the right tone to pick and connected to the feelings of people in London and across the country on that day. It is an excellent illustration too of the value of understanding human emotions when you think about what to do or say next. Business has a predominance of the Myers Briggs 'Thinking' preference. In fact, from my experience, I would say that at least 75 per cent of the business people that I have met (and whose MBTI profile I have known) possess the 'Thinking' preference. I would also say that they slip into the rational mode of thinking with the ease of a penguin into the cold, black sea.

The dominance of the rational thinking model is such a puzzle for me. Let us, for a moment, think about some of the biggest and most important decisions we take in life. They might include who we choose to marry or live with, what house or car we buy, the friends we make, whether to have children, or even where to go on holiday. All of these are important decisions; many of them are very costly and all of them require considerable planning. However, who you fall in love with tends not to be determined by a rational evaluation of the options; the friends that you make and keep arises from how you feel when in the company of those friends; the last house that you bought probably just felt good – maybe it was light and airy or made you feel safe; your holiday destinations probably tap into your need for excitement and exploration. Whatever the reasons and whatever the motivation it is clear that in big important life decisions while rationality is of course part of our thinking process, matters of the heart have an equal if not larger role to play.

Why, then, in business and in organizations which both employ people and typically deliver products and services to people, is feeling and emotional state rarely factored in to the thinking process? Worse still, why is it regarded by many as a second order question? The thinking being: let's get the system or the design right first and then think about the people in the system. It just seems crazy.

I once participated in a development program along with senior figures from a mix of management consultancies. The aim of the program was to help develop the skills of consultants working at board level. Much of the focus was on how to build relationships in order to become a 'trusted advisor' and to do so by helping to shift the thinking of the board-level player to a better place. The activity took the form of a classic developmental method to teach coaching. In this scenario, there was a coach, a problem-holder (the coachee), a series of observers each with different roles, and a trained facilitator. After each session, usually lasting 30–45 min, the participants would switch roles and keep doing so until, with the guidance of the facilitator, the learning was well and truly absorbed. One particular session offered some fascinating insights and went a little like this:

Coach: So David, it would be good if you could we could talk about some of the challenges you're facing at the moment.

Coachee: Well, we've had a very difficult time of late with a company to which we sub-contracted a major piece of audit work to undertake on our behalf and frankly they have made a mess of it. They've been bullish and not really understood the client's business. They haven't built any trust at any level, and as a result, they've annoyed the client and this has been brought to the attention of the Audit Committee that has made us look bad too.

Coach: And this has generated some specific problems for you?

Coachee: Absolutely, not least because I stuck my neck out and deliberately selected this company because I recognized that they would be tough and would place high expectations on the client. I am very keen to bring this client into the 21st century and this company was a perfect way to do this.

Coach: Have you raised this with the partner in the sub-contracted firm?

Coachee: Yes, we've been very straight with them. We've made it clear that they have handled it badly. It's been difficult for me though because I have been a strong supporter of the high standards that they operate.

Coach: You mentioned the Audit Committee. How displeased were they?

Coachee: They were livid. They are a strong Audit Committee and of course they represent all of the top-level players that we need to work with. We need to win their respect and this is very embarrassing.

Coach: Could you arrange for another partner to take client responsibility to replace the current partner?

Coachee: Well we could I suppose, but we are already committed and it may look even worse for us if we changed tack now. Besides they are the right firm and it's the right partner for the job, it is just that they've started very badly and have damaged our reputation in the process

Coach: At what point in the process was it apparent to you that things were going wrong?

Coachee: I think we first heard some murmurings from the Finance Director a couple of months ago. It was in a meeting about an entirely different matter and he made a couple of cryptic comments about the contractor. I didn't understand them at the time, but in retrospect, I suppose I should have pursued them.

The process continued for some time, seeming to find no way forward until the facilitator intervened to halt the session. Before she commenced the review, however, she invited the coachee to stay in role and asked them one question: 'it sounds like you have a lot personally invested in this. You clearly care about the helping the client a great deal and, in many ways, you've put your own reputation on the line to do this. How must that feel?' The question provoked a stunning response. The coachee looked as if a huge weight had been lifted from their shoulders. His eyes teared a little and he nodded furiously in recognition spilling out a river of feelings on the subject. It transpired that the coachee felt incredibly alone; that he knew that he had made the right decision to select the contractor and should hold his nerve but he had been plagued with doubts; the coachee also explored whether the client too, and even the Audit Committee may have unexpressed feelings about the new arrangements and the new world. At the conclusion of the session, the coachee left the room clear about the way forward and energized to take action.

In short, the rational model of inquiry was never going to move the thinking of the coachee forward. His feelings on the subject were a critical component of the problem and the process of searching and offering hypotheses in the rational mode may never have got to the solution. Looking back on the events, it was crystal clear to that coach that the coachee was flagging up the issues from the outset. His references to personal risk and various feelings of embarrassment and doubt couldn't have been better articulated. Sadly, because of the limitations of using the rational model, they were falling on deaf ears.

This example illustrates something else for us too. It offers a particular pattern that is common to rational thinking whenever an individual (or group) is engaged in problem solving. It might be in providing mentoring advice to a colleague or solving some difficulties in another part of the business. In the example the coach, in their hunger to help, treated the problem as if it were a broken engine. In order to diagnose what needed to happen next, the coachee systematically selected a series of diagnostic questions that he thought would deliver the information he needed to come up with the right answer; almost as if once he knew as much as the coachee he would, of course, see the light. I call this subset of rational thinking 'information grab'. It's a bit like playing the popular children's game 'Animal, Vegetable, Mineral', where the aim is to guess, using 20 questions, which animal, mineral, or vegetable the other person is thinking. Questions can only be answered with 'yes' or 'no' and sooner or later, the options will have been narrowed to the point where the answer is obvious.

In more complex situations, where the process of thinking is inextricably bound to the decisions reached, we have to be a little more sophisticated. Firstly, the rational model, by definition, tends not to view feelings as relevant data to the problem in-hand. Secondly, problems are rarely solved by simply possessing all of the 'relevant' facts. If that were the case, then in the example used the coachee wouldn't need any help. It is, of course, the insights you bring to those facts that make the difference. Thirdly, as a recipient of the 'information grab' approach (assuming you are dealing with people rather than conducting paper-based research), you feel disempowered, less ownership of the issues as you pass them to another and you feel like a dry husk once every droplet of information has been sucked out of you. After that, the problem-solver needs to come up with some pretty amazing solutions to have made the process worthwhile.

As you observe interactions between people at work or elsewhere, consider how much time is spent in rational mode as compared to exploring feelings, values, or personal motivations. Watch what happens to the advancement of thinking on the occasions feelings are tapped into.

Sticky Thinking

Have you ever noticed that, despite how much you can find a pop song annoying, repetitive, and puerile, you catch yourself one day, perhaps walking around a grocery store, humming it? The second most comforting thing in this is that you are not alone in having this experience; the first is that you will probably have inadvertently passed it on to someone else and, as you pass the meats counter, you will hear another poor victim whistling the tune. It's as if as soon as something catches your attention it sticks to your mind like a Post-It note and it takes quite some effort to shake it off.

In conversations too this happens frequently and with great rapidity. It might be a meeting of the board to discuss the prospect of downsizing unprofitable areas of the business. As an aside, someone briefly mentions some difficulties in recruiting local graduates at the Edinburgh branch. Someone at the table expresses concern as the London offices have a surfeit of graduate applications. The discussion leads in to the challenge of differentiating higher performing universities from poorer universities. The Finance Director comments that when he left university and joined the company, there was a lower company requirement for degree performance: 'A second class degree in those days was perfectly acceptable'. The Human Resources Director adds that not only have the entrance requirements risen, the entry assessment procedures have become considerably tougher. A colleague reflects that while the organizational changes have made entrance assessment more stringent, the new performance appraisal system for existing staff, with its new relative assessment regime, has caused considerable distress among some staff that feel the system is unduly harsh and unfair. A colleague raises the point that this has knocked the confidence of many middle managers as subjects and administrators of the system. They are desperately trying to motivate people at a time of rapid change only to have a new, highly critical system to implement. 'Our middle managers are the workhorse of the organization' says the Chief Executive Officer, 'this needs our urgent attention!' Before the group know it, 30 minutes have passed, large amounts of money spent in senior staff time, and no headway has been made on the original proposition for the meeting. Table 1.2 represents the sequence of events.

Table 1.2 Illustration of Sticky Thinking

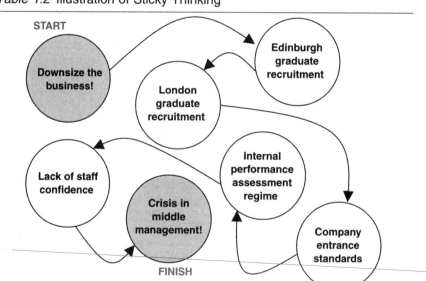

Sticky Thinking is not always contained to single conversations. In some cases, sticky thoughts can stay with us for days. A friend of mine had a boss that suffered from, as my friend joked, 'impression-in-a-pillow' syndrome, which referred to his apparent compulsion to be unduly influenced by conversations he had had a few days earlier (like an impression left in a pillow). One example was when his boss had met a senior figure whose background was in marketing. They had clearly touched on the subject of market segmentation and so at almost every opportunity, and even when it wasn't terribly appropriate, the prospect of segmenting the market would be applied to: the groupings that made up society, the internal customers within the organization, the division of books in the library. If you wanted to be in the favor of the boss that week, mentioning market segmentation would significantly raise your stock. Next week though, after the boss had met with a leading academic who spoke of 'operationalizing' social theories, i.e. turning theory into practice, being better at delivery was *really about* operationalizing the concept of 'earned value management'; cost cutting was about operationalizing the 'theory of constraints'.

This is different though from having a pet subject or more seriously having principles and insights that you want to bring to the table (principles that you may offer repeatedly to help to advance thinking). By Sticky Thinking, I mean those interactions where we find the conversation wandering, through associations, from one subject to another. And this is a very serious and real issue on which to focus. Research conducted by MCI Worldcom into the time we spend in meetings highlights some startling results.

UK businesses waste enormous amounts of time and money on unproductive meetings, according to recent research. The research, commissioned by MCI WorldCom Conferencing and carried out by the Research Business International, finds the typical busy professional attends nearly 60 meetings a month, of which more than 10 per cent involve travel out of town. A typical out-of-town six-person meeting costs £1,645. This includes significant "soft" costs, such as lost productivity while participants are travelling to and arranging meetings, which must be considered for a true evaluation of meetings.

"Meetings in the UK: a study of trends, costs and attitudes towards business travel and teleconferencing, and their impact on productivity" draws on the government's Office for National Statistics' Labour Force Survey and the meeting habits of more than 400 professionals in middle and senior management positions … This research reveals that heavy meeting-goers find it difficult to maintain their commitments: 87 per cent have missed meetings, 80 per cent have daydreamed and 23 per cent have dozed off during meetings. Travelling to meetings also affects professionals' welfare: 28 per cent say they are more stressed when travelling to meetings, with 50 per cent saying they are concerned about work piling up while they are away.

In the United States, according to the Wall Street Journal's report on Wharton Centre For Applied Research (November 2004):

The average CEO in the United States spends 17 hours a week in meetings that cost the company $42,500 per year. Senior executives spend 23 hours a week in meetings and cost up to $46,000 per year each. Middle managers spend 11 hours a week in meetings and cost up to $20,000 a year each

Taking these statistics alone and imagining even a small organization comprised of 1,000 staff and, lets say, one Chief Executive Officer, 50 senior executives, and 120 middle managers, we would expect the company to spend $4.7m each year attending meetings, and this excludes the cost incurred in meetings by the remaining 829 members of staff below middle manager. Highlighting the significance of the point, there are numerous products available on the market, and many via the Internet, which provide quick calculations of the cost of company meetings. In fact, some companies offer to install digital recording equipment that will automatically capture, calculate, and disseminate the costs of meetings as they take place. Dramatic reductions in meeting costs have been reported where this has taken place.

In the next meeting you attend, draw a series of circles on a piece of paper and each time the conversation shifts in focus, write down a two or three word description in each bubble. When you get to the end of the meeting, observe how often shifts in thinking are influenced by the associations people make rather than the contribution that can be made to the problem in hand.

Common Sense Thinking

Common sense is another thinking habit of ours that possesses enormous power. It involves applying general principles often taken from experience or borrowed from similar situations to bring help to a problem or challenge. It is an approach that draws heavily on the rational model and, in particular, it makes good use of logical deduction and logical induction. However, as with all of our habits, we rarely pause to think whether it is fit for purpose; whether in fact, common sense is good enough.

The American Independence advocate Thomas Paine, along with most dictionary definitions, describes common sense as 'beliefs or propositions that seem, to most people, to be prudent and of sound judgment'. Other definitions refer to 'conventional wisdom', 'native good judgment', or 'practical sense'. What is well recognized is that common sense does not rely on expert or specialized knowledge, rather it is something of a numbers game – the more people that hold a view, the more commonly held that view is, the more we can ascribe the descriptor of common sense to that view.

I do not wish to give the impression that popular perspectives are lacking. The wonderful book *The Wisdom of Crowds* by James Surowiecki beautifully illuminates the value of common-thought. He starts his book with the popular TV quiz show *Who Wants to be a Millionaire?* and, in reference to the 'ask the audience' option available to all contestants, he argues that where individual thought is pitted against group intelligence, the group will always win; the popular, commonly held sense will always win through.

The Delphi technique, used by the RAND Corporation since the late 1960s, added another dimension to the notion of common sense by providing a methodology for assembling experts across different but related subject areas, to reach consensus – a common view – on key decisions. One application of the technique involves inviting a group of people to answer a question that may be unrelated to their specialities. For example, it might be to ask a group of zoo keepers 'how many cars are manufactured in Japan each year?' Individually each participant would write his or her estimate on a Post-It. After each round, the estimates would be shared with the group and then the process repeated again. The combined contribution and subsequent adjustments to estimates would, over time, lead the group to an accurate prediction. It's a fascinating method that delivers startling results.

In companies across the world we have seen, in increasing numbers, much greater use of large group problem-solving; and not just group processes as a means to 'buy-in' staff to the latest management edict. Groups have been engaged in activities that had previously been firmly in the domain of the top team – strategy formulation, determining the organization's vision, and even major decisions about growth and contraction. Organizations doing this have been as diverse as BBC who have engaged literally thousands of employees in the business of the Corporation and Nokia phones in Finland. The program of activity in each case has been to draw upon and build common sense ideas about how to take organizations forward.

Common sense is good and it works well for us, particularly where explicit thought has been given, in the case of the Delphi technique and the facilitation methodologies that accompany large group work, to how best to tap into common sense. The area, though, that needs greatest attention is in the habit of common sense – the day-to-day setting where common sense too often rules supreme.

My interest in leadership has grown over the years, not only from a professional perspective, but also on a much deeper level. It is a subject that fascinates me for its complexity, it's joining of the personal and the business and for the way it has as many expert commentators as it does common-sense commentators. Leadership development, and in fact all training and development, is the same – everyone seems to have a view (unfortunately often negative). With history and more immediately our TV screens littered with magnificent leaders such as Nelson Mandela, Winston Churchill, and Gandhi people feel as inclined to offer their wisdom on leadership as easily as they might talk about the latest TV program or the weather.

My role in designing leadership development experiences has engendered within me quite an acute sense of the difference between what sounds right and what works – often two entirely different things. It sounds right to many of us that being intelligent, that having high standards and being charismatic will help to make a good leader. Maybe even showing 110 per cent commitment to the cause will help too. These are common-sense judgments about what matters. Equally, in terms of development activities it sounds right too that emerging leaders will benefit from teaching by the finest academics and practitioners available. Perhaps the training format could be a speaking session from an academic followed by a 'Q & A'. To denote the importance of this maybe too some sessions should be held over dinner. Again, these are common sense notions of what seems right.

In the examples used here, there is good reason to challenge all of the common sense notions of what constitutes good leadership and to firmly question the design of appropriate interventions. Let us explore in a little detail some of the common sense ingredients of leadership:

Intelligence   Intelligence is clearly an important pre-requisite for operating at a senior level in any organization. However, it is important to explore what kind of intelligence leaders might need in order to help the organization to be successful. There are numerous models that seek to capture different dimensions of intelligence, but I would like to refer to two types of intelligence that are quite different but very important. The first, Emotional Intelligence, is now very well understood and was brought to public attention through Daniel Goleman's book of the same name, published in 1995. Goleman brought together research from different fields that convincingly argued that IQ is not a good predictor of job performance. Instead, our ability to handle frustration, control emotions, and get along with other people seemed to matter more. Research originally conducted at Berkeley University in the 1950s and then repeated 40 years later concluded that social and emotional abilities were four times more important than IQ in determining professional success and prestige. For all of the emphasis our education system and our recruitment processes in business have given to more conventional forms of intelligence, this groundbreaking work concluded that common sense, in deducing that IQ was of primary importance, had failed us.

The second form of intelligence is highlighted by the work of Harry Schroeder formerly of Princeton University, New Jersey and developed by Tony Cockerill formerly of London Business School. This work offered the term 'conceptual flexibility' as one of three crucial ingredients in thinking for leaders. It refers to an ability to assimilate complex and often conflicting data; to be able to simultaneously adopt different perspectives on a subject and to accommodate those perspectives into the way we see the world. It is a very modern way of thinking and encourages us to see the part (perhaps of a business) and the whole at the same time. It invites us to see interconnectedness and to value alternative perspectives. It is a form of thinking that, in many ways, is not common to us. The important point here is that the research shows that it is this (and the previous example of emotional intelligence) that leads to results in business and without properly understanding what you mean by intelligence, or without having a firm basis to believe that the input variable leads to the desired outcome, your views, as sensible as they seem, are no more than speculation.

Charisma

The research undertaken by James Collins and Jerry Porras and published in 1994 in their book Built to Last is now well known. Jim Collins proposed that, despite the commonly held notion that charisma is essential to leadership, it could in fact be the death knell for an organization. Their research looked to companies in the United States that had prospered over time and had, over decades, been sustainable and continually on top of their game. He then looked to the characteristics of the chief executives to find that those companies with the greatest staying power had a mixture of leaders, very few of whom could be described as charismatic. His work had surprised and challenged pre-conceptions about what made for good leadership.

High standards and having 110 per cent commitment

These final categories appear on the face of it to be sensible. Who could argue with the position that having high standards would improve performance; who could disagree that 110 per cent commitment would help? In many ways, experience tells us that possessing these qualities can mean trouble. Both of these qualities are strongly associated with a pacesetting style of leadership where the leader expects a lot of their staff. Leaders with this style can be highly critical of below (their) standard performance, can tend to micro-manage and create an organizational climate that is judged by staff to be constraining and damaging in the long term. A typical picture is performance that rises initially, but drops sharply once the pressure is off. Leadership then takes a hit in terms of loyalty and staff tend to feel managed rather than led. In short, the qualities listed can sound right but very often they don't deliver results.

Academic or practitioner teaching followed by 'Q & A'

It is a classic developmental design to have speaker input followed by a Q & A. It is entirely understandable too that so many leadership development interventions take this form. While being commonly held as the way to teach leadership, it can be so wide of the mark in achieving any shift in learning or performance.

The point of reference for this design is typically school or university where the 'chalk and talk' style is normal business. The problem of course is that the school and university environment is focused on passing down knowledge to students who seek to make sense of the lessons. In the world of leadership, certainly in my experience, the area that almost always needs most attention is behavioral change, not intellectual topping-up. The habit can be very hard to break but sees millions of pounds each year poorly spent and business results barely touched

This is, of course, one example of how Common Sense Thinking can find its way into places it shouldn't be. But in my experience, I see common sense being used too much in organizations and people with generalist abilities turning their hands to anything from marketing to finance or from client management to IT systems. And even within such disciplines, general experience and the thinking that goes with it too often replaces insight and demonstrable expertise.

There is a delightful quotation used by the educationalist John Dewey in his book *How We Think* first published in 1910:

The story is told of a man in slight repute for intelligence, who, desiring to be chosen selectman in his New England town, addressed a knot of neighbours in this wise way 'I hear you don't believe I know enough to hold office. I wish you to understand that I am thinking about something or other most of the time' (p. 2)

As you speak to colleagues and friends about any topic over the next few weeks, ask yourself how they know what they are saying. Question whether they are offering views born of knowledge, or expertise, or common sense. Think too which particular arms of the business in which you work are viewed as more susceptible to Common Sense Thinking and consider relative to your own area of the business how true this might be?

Binary Thinking

The word 'binary' describes a system that has only two possible options or digits, normally 0 and 1. It is a system that is essential in technology and underpins the processing protocol in all modern computers. The thinking behind this relates to electrical circuitry that can have only two possible states, either on or off. A simple example is the light in a room that can either be turned on or off – there is no in-between point, and the selection of one of the two options available excludes the other from being possible. It is in the combination and sequencing of binary coding that technological systems can deliver such immense processing power.

I use the principle of a binary system as a metaphor to explore another of our dominant thinking habits – Binary Thinking.

In almost every activity of life I see the broader principles of Binary Thinking being reflected. In human biology, the heart works by contracting and pumping blood around the body, and then relaxing to allow blood to enter the heart. This binary action, almost like a light turned on and off, is repeated for the rest of our lives. Our lungs do the same. As we breathe in, our lungs inflate and oxygen is extracted from the air; and as we breathe out, carbon dioxide is expelled from the body. Neither can, nor should, happen at the same time. In sport, the competition between two players whether boxing or tennis or even chess relies on a binary principle of either/or. I win or you win; it simply can't be both. In accountancy, the principle of double-entry bookkeeping requires that a transaction be denoted as either a debit or a credit. Even its counter-entry has to follow the same rule. In criminal law, judgements are based on guilt or innocence. In movies we have good and evil. And in war we have enemies and allies.

It is no surprise at all that our method of thinking too has a binary component to it. Binary Thinking is of great value when we truly believe that the most appropriate way to represent the problems or solutions that we face is to conceive of two, mutually exclusive options. A typical characterization of problems/possibilities that we face is outlined in Table 1.3.

Table 1.3 Typical characterizations of binary problems/possibilities

To innovate	To be conservative
To centralize decision-making	To devolve decision-making
To change	To stay as we are
To be autocratic	To be democratic
To grow	To contract
To lead	To follow
To be quick	To be slow
To do it ourselves	To sub-contract

Over the years, I have worked with a range of executive coaches, many of whom have also provided career counseling for senior executives who feel that they have come to a crossroads in their lives. I am reminded of one occasion on which I wanted to test out the skills of a particular executive coach, and to do so I asked if they would be willing to explore the career options that I once had. This was quite some time ago, when I had assumed that I would want a career with a path that took me towards working for a large multi-national perhaps in the field of consultancy. The session was informed by an exercise that I undertook alone to identify the times in my life, whether in work or elsewhere, when I was in 'flow'. The concept of 'flow' was developed by Mihaly Csikszentmihalyi, a psychology professor at the University of Chicago, who proposed that optimal performance in all of us occurs at a time when we are fully immersed in an activity to the point that we achieve an almost Zen like sense of oneness with that activity. In such a mental state, time flies by, there is a falling away of ego and there is a great sense of achievement. In lay terms, this has been described as 'being in the zone' and 'in the groove', and it provides an excellent basis on which to explore future career decisions.

In the rather lengthy experiences that I described, of which I first couldn't make sense, I was struck by what seemed to be an extraordinary pattern of events. The first was my love for SCUBA diving that I described as a 'flow' activity because of the way in which it was a total experience that gave me a sense of absolute freedom along with absolute responsibility for my well being. I talked about the need for moment-to-moment alertness of my body movement in the water, the shifts in current, the air tank that I needed to monitor, and the necessity to communicate without words but with complete clarity to fellow divers. I also wrote about the apparent chaos of fish society that, as I came to know it better, I appreciated was highly ordered. Fish would literally queue, like at a barbershop, in order to have barnacles and debris removed from their scales by an attendant cleaner wrasse. Remoras would swim with sharks to clean their sandpaper skins with the reward of occasional scraps of food. The synergy was a joy to watch. Another 'flow' experience was the time I spent writing a thesis on the culture of organizations. This was a hefty piece of work and took me some six months to write. I described my 'flow' experience as one where, within a bounded time period, I had freedom to focus and craft the thesis as I saw fit. One the one hand, whatever I saw as being germane to the subject I could introduce or research further. Whatever theory or methodology I thought was useful came under my gaze. On the other hand, I paid regular attention to the conventions of the work, the sociological discipline to which I was working and the pressure to deliver something on time, to a fixed word count and to an externally applied standard.

The quandary that I found myself in when I reviewed these and other 'flow' moments was that they appeared contradictory. I appeared to revel in freedom and to be more alive then I ever was when I was my own boss. But at the same time, all of my flow experiences took place where the setting was bounded and constrained. In my SCUBA diving example, my experience was limited by available air in the tank. In my thesis example, the work was subject to stiff external standards, to a rigid word limit and to a time deadline. The pleasure I derived from exploring the apparent chaos of the underwater world was matched by the pleasure I felt when I understood that in fact the chaos was order; that fish were members of a society with norms not unlike human society. I concluded with some discomfort that I was most alive and effective when I could innovate and be free, but also when I had to follow the rules and be constrained.

At the time I had accepted these as contradictions and I pondered for quite a while what they meant. With the help of the executive coach, I came to appreciate that these were not contradictory at all; they weren't mutually exclusive, paradoxical, or inconsistent. Above all, they were not, as I had imagined before that time, either/or options. If I were to steer my career choices based on my flow preferences, it was simply a matter of finding organizations and positions where within an established and strong structure, perhaps even a traditional organization, I would be allowed space to operate and the freedom to innovate. And, as I discovered, there were and are a surprising number that fit the description.

Returning to Table 1.3 and its typical characterizations of binary options, I cannot tell you how many times I have heard these apparent inconsistencies being presented as either/or possibilities. I imagine, too, that in your daily lives you hear them being routinely mentioned. Dr Barry Johnson has undertaken a wealth of excellent work in this area under the heading of Polarity Management. His work forms an important distinction between 'problems' which he explains may be solved by single solutions (that may fall on either side of a binary division) and 'polarities' which are interdependent variables and, as such, any change to one will affect the other. For example, experience tells us that the likely outcome of centralizing decision-making will, over time, be the corrosion of local responsibility, local knowledge, local client relationships and place closeness to customers at risk. The consequence being that if you wait long enough there will be a call to return to devolved decision-making to counterbalance the downside of central control. Wait for another few years and the pendulum will swing right back. Barry's truly insightful thinking and methodology proposes designing systems that will hold on to the benefits of both poles without dipping down into the weaknesses of both sides.

In this book, I make a slightly less sophisticated point. My view is that we have developed this form of Binary Thinking into a habit so that it is seen as normal and, as such, it is left unchecked. We take for granted the notion that it is sensible to formulate problems or possibilities into seemingly mutually exclusive camps. At a more fundamental level, we also take it for granted that if we have gone through the steps of identifying two distinct and different options to help meet our challenges, we have done the thinking needed to solve our problems. What we have actually done is sleepwalked our way into working with a reduced range of possibilities and conned ourselves into thinking that a combination of both, even if they are genuinely our best option, is not possible.

The next time you are in a brainstorming session or are in a group called upon to solve problems, listen to the way Binary Thinking is used. Each time you hear an either/or option being presented, ask yourself whether in fact the two options might be combined. Ask yourself whether enough thinking has been done to weed out the abundance of solutions to the problem. Before you put this book down, think about under what circumstances it might be possible to achieve both of the binary options in all the examples in Table 1.3.

Equity Thinking

Closely related to the families of deficit and rational thinking is the final category of Equity Thinking; an incredibly dominant habit of ours that refers to the principle of fairness as a quiet but powerful engine in our thinking processes. Such is the strength of this human predilection that if you search on the Internet to find references to the following keyword searches you get a sense of how important fairness and equity are in our thinking[2]:

fair[3]	85.5 million hits
equality	20.4 million hits
unfair	13.6 million hits
equity[4]	11.8 million hits

fairness   11.3 million hits
inequality   8.5 million hits
accountancy   4.1 million hits
(for comparative purposes)

When we think about equity and fairness we are reminded of how tightly tied-in these principles are to our notions of civilized society. From a philosophical and from a moral perspective, it is difficult to think of fairness as being anything other than 'right'. Our language, our legal system, our social system, even our attitude to conflict sees a playing out of Equity Thinking. Just consider some of the words and phrases commonly found in our vocabulary – equality of opportunity, meritocracy, gender equality, fair trade, copyright fair use, equal pay, 'a level playing field', fairness doctrine, 'true and fair financial accounts', 'fair share', 'fair dues', social justice, racial equality, 'equality of access', 'unfair discrimination', 'inequalities in health care', 'all's fair in love and war', equal rights, 'all men are created equal', 'all animals are equal', and equal treatment.

In practice, Equity Thinking involves making direct comparisons between two or more like-events or groups with the expectation that there should be an equal distribution of a particular variable such as legal rights, opportunity, funds, health, power, voice, access, or behavior. It is in the application of this principle and the moral force that it carries that almost every social movement in the last century – from voting rights for women to gay rights – has made headway. Invoking the principle of fairness coupled with tireless campaigning and legislative changes, and more often than not, direct action, has made possible all that we now accept and hold as 'right'.

To illustrate the power of Equity Thinking in a slightly different way, ask yourself the question: what case might have been put to make these advances if the principle of fairness had not existed? How much more difficult would the struggle of the suffragettes have been if they could not have pointed to the inequality between men and women on voting rights? How much more difficult would it have been to have affected changes to the employment rights of ethnic minorities across North America and Europe if differential treatment between white and non-white employees was deemed acceptable? Within the healthcare system, what case would have been put to prevent wealthier patients being treated more quickly than poorer patients if not the principle of equity?

As with all our other thinking habits, Equity Thinking is superb and without it we would be far less able to tackle the challenges we face. As a habit though, as with all habits, we follow the equity path unthinkingly – equating fair thinking with optimal thinking; automatically focusing on what seems fair instead of fully understanding what works. As participants and observers to Equity Thinking we also complicitly reinforce the 'rightness' of looking for opportunities to even things up; using our eye for deficiencies to agree that something seems unbalanced or out of place.

Just the other day, I was sitting in a restaurant and overheard a bizarre conversation between a young couple who were whispering loudly to one another. The couple were desperate not to make a scene but even more determined to get their seemingly conflicting views across. Initially, I imagined that it was quite serious until I heard a few words drifting across to, by now, my highly attuned ears. Curiously it transpired that they were arguing about the food they had ordered. They had both ordered foie gras and chicken terrine as a starter and were struck by how different the proportion of foie gras to chicken appeared to be in each of their terrines. The woman had less foie gras than the man. Neither had yet tasted the starter but the scene was nevertheless well underway. As the somewhat strange story unfolded, it became clear that this wasn't the first time that the woman had been given less of what she had most liked about her order in a restaurant. 'It's not fair. This always happens to me', the whispering complaint drifted across the room. 'Well why don't you have mine then?' he replied, attempting to quietly but firmly switch plates. 'That wouldn't be fair on you either', she replied switching them back just as quickly. It was a fairness stalemate. They sat staring at each other as the whispering-shouting ceased.

For me, it was a wonderful illustration of two serious questions about Equity Thinking. Firstly, whose perspective do you consider the issue of fairness? Secondly, is fairness always a useful principle to apply? In the case of the restaurant inequity neither diner knew whether their starter tasted better with a greater or lesser proportion of foie gras. The female diner might ironically have benefited more from an inequitable distribution.

An organizational illustration of both these issues is when I worked in organization where, among other things, I had overall responsibility for approximately 200 accountancy trainees that would work and train with the organization. They would each participate in a 40-month training program that would eventually lead them to Chartered Accountancy status with strong career prospects for the rest of their lives. It was a tough qualification and was fairly unrelenting in the frequency of exams and assessments. The organization had clearly laid down policy on the various exam performances that students had to attain in order to progress to each stage and to stay in the employ of the organization. Over the years, we had built data on the extent to which relatively poorer exam performances at early stages in the training program were predictive of final stage failure rates. After evaluating the position and reflecting on our existing policy and consulting too with other companies who trained accountants, we took the decision to raise the organizational pass rate by a few but significant notches for subsequent intakes of graduates.

This met with a barrage of complaints from trainees, their managers, and their 'counseling directors' who forcibly challenged the decision on the grounds that it was inequitable to expect trainees studying only a year or more apart to be subject to different assessment regimes. Many managers and counseling directors had too passed through the system some years before and could sympathize with the stringency of the new arrangements. Inevitably, as students began to filter through the new regime, some students fell short by a couple of marks which, under the old policy, would have been sufficient for them to pass through the gateway to the next stage. In these cases, however, contracts were required to be terminated and again trainees, managers, and counseling directors all put the case that it was an unfair system. Not only, though, were trainees and their supporters as one in the view that the system was unfair, but their fellow students who had passed under the new regime held the same line. At times, the organization had most of the 200 trainees disgruntled and opposed to the arrangement. Worst still, in a very buoyant marketplace where more than two-thirds of trainees would leave the organization within two years of qualification, the level of dissatisfaction borne from this sense of inequity threatened to strip the organization of almost all its qualifying trainees, which had represented a heavy financial investment. It was a serious problem.

On the question, though, of 'fair to whom?' there are a great many ways of seeing this situation and Table 1.4 points to some of the main perspectives from which this question might be answered.

In the example given, the perspective that came to the fore was that of the trainee and, in particular, those trainees that were subject to a different exam policy from previous years. From this viewpoint, it is entirely understandable that the new arrangements could be understood as unfair, particularly as students met socially and worked alongside trainees from different years who were subject to lower standards of assessment. However, if we shift our attention to students only within each year, the picture looks more equitable. Every student, for

Table 1.4 The equity principle as viewed from different perspectives

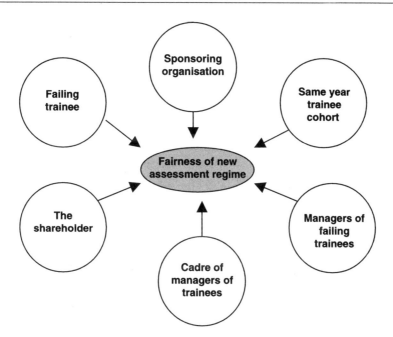

example in a single year's intake, would join the organization on an explicit understanding of the performance standards required and would sign up to the 40-month contract on that basis.

From the perspective of the organization, it needs to protect its investment and, if empirical research shows that those trainees who initially 'squeeze through' against a weaker standard run a higher risk of failing two or three years down the line, then to be fair to the sponsoring organization, it is justified in raising the bar. Furthermore, if the organization makes the standard an explicit term of the contract at the outset, then it would be unfair of the employee to accuse the organization of operating an unfair system.

Managers of failing trainees may view the system as unfair because they will, at least temporarily, lose staff as their contracts are terminated. At least in the short-term, such managers can feel as much a victim of the new system as the trainees. However, there is no doubt that it is only through chance that a manager may have a failed trainee working for them and because the distribution of trainees is random (within the organization illustrated), the system cannot be held to be unfair even if, for example, the same manager were to year after year receive trainees that failed. That would just be bad luck not inequitable.

Moving clockwise around the circle in Table 1.4, it is clear that fairness, viewed from different perspectives, can cause a 180-degree shift in thinking and in the prevailing view. Taking the shareholder as our last illustration, the first point that needs to be made is that, as the ultimate sponsor of this organization's services, this is a viewpoint that can't afford to be ignored or underemphasized. It is in the shareholders' interest that resources should be invested well, and it is only fair to the shareholder that judgments on the way their money is spent is based on sound investment decisions. If every year, or even every six months, the exam pass level rate were to change perhaps to keep pace with changing standards or even stronger predictive data, then, from the shareholders' perspective, this too would be fair because it would represent an equitable return on the investment made.

This brings me to my second point about Equity Thinking which is that so often it is used out of place – not even consciously; maybe even compulsively at times. In the example above, the concept of equity is important but it should be way down the list in considering how best to employees with the skills needed to best serve customers. That is where the focus of thinking should be.

Keep your ears pricked for Equity Thinking. Try to see how early on in a conversation you can detect someone forming comparisons in order to find inconsistencies, and ultimately to conclude that something is unfair. If you wish to be devilish, ask them why fairness is important. Ask them too whether there are other legitimate comparisons that haven't been made and why this is so.

A bleak summary

At this point, I would like to provide a brief summary of the shortcomings of the thinking habits we use. I am aware in doing this that this is a deficit-focused approach, but I am using this strategy for two reasons. Firstly, because our thinking styles are well used thinking habits, we automatically assume they are a sensible way to think, and I want to remind you why this is not always the case. In doing so, I hope to open up some other ways of thinking that we might incorporate within our repertoire. These are explored later. Secondly, in the remainder of this and the next chapter, I want to move on to a more sociological perspective which requires us to think about both the processes through which habits are formed, and the impact this has on the way we make sense of the world. In order to do this, I need to bring each thinking style back on to the radar, warts-and-all as follows:

With **Deficit Thinking** – we reduce all of human existence to a tangle of problems.

With **Rational Thinking** – we exclude the importance of human emotions in how we make decisions.

With **Sticky Thinking** – we allow random thoughts to direct our analysis.

With **Common Sense Thinking** – we settle for inexpert knowledge in place of real understanding.

With **Binary Thinking** – we oversimplify and 'dumb down' our analysis of the world we live in.

With **Equity Thinking** – we reduce all analysis to a game of 'Snap'[5].

The production and shaping of thinking habits

In order for any form of behavior to become a habit, it needs, in the process of repeated usage, to deliver a net benefit to the actor, otherwise the habit would be discarded. Benefits, however, can come in many shapes and even some of our less savory habits, such as leaving the top off the toothpaste tube or riding the clutch in a car, provide us with an advantage. The advantage is that of efficiency. It makes our lives considerably more straightforward and energy-efficient if we can rely on established patterns of behavior whenever we face similar situations. This is good because across the landscape of mundane tasks that we have to perform on a daily basis, we don't really need to think twice about how to do something. In fact, we don't even want to have to think once. If we have a way of doing something that seems to work then that's good enough; it may not be the very best way, but if it works, it works.

However, when we are dealing with more serious habits we might want to think again about what is going on in their reproduction, and to consider where they lead us. For example, we can get into trouble when our habits become hardened to the point where, even though we might want to change our behavior, we always slip back into the same pattern. There are often conditions or triggers too, in the environment, that encourage us to stick with our habits. For many years, before I read a simply fantastic book by Allen Carr called *Easy Way to Stop Smoking*, I would always reach for a cigarette whenever (a) I was having an alcoholic drink, (b) after a main meal, (c) when I drank coffee, or (d) when I was around other smokers. A pattern, I suspect, that is not dissimilar to a great many smokers. Thanks to Allen Carr, I haven't smoked for a number of years, and the breaking of this particular habit as well as the addiction will certainly have added years to my life.

Thinking habits are no less important; in fact they are the means by which we navigate our way through life. In the same way that we think about the factors that influence smoking, our thinking habits too are triggered and shaped by the environment and behaviors of others. Not only do our thinking styles themselves possess positive and negative qualities that we rarely pause to consider, but our adoption of particular thinking styles, in any given situation, is driven by factors that remain largely invisible to us. This lack of self-awareness and bondage to our circumstance is not a strategy that should prepare us for the challenges we are likely to face in the 21st century.

How thinking habits can be shaped in group settings

Much of our thinking is done in groups. It is a setting where thinking habits are often formed and shown to be the 'right' way to behave. If you are a leader, a senior figure, if you chair meetings, if you facilitate thinking processes, if in any way you are a participant in group work you will have, perhaps unwittingly, helped to construct normative thinking behavior and to have shaped the thinking habits of those around you. Your complicity, each time thinking behavior is repeated, serves to represent that behavior as the 'norm'; your use of specific thinking habits sends the message to other participants that this is a legitimate way to think; and your personal success in deploying particular thinking styles markets that style to others.

Each of our thinking habits can be introduced and supported by different triggers. Using Sticky Thinking, we can see in Table 1.5 an illustration of some of the factors that can bring the habit into usage and help to establish it as a 'norm'.

The general theme that we can draw from the environment that supports Sticky Thinking is that where group conversations lack

Table 1.5 An illustration of key triggers and shapers of Sticky Thinking

Thinking habit	Key triggers that have particularly 'sticky' properties	Key triggers that create an environment for Sticky Thinking
Sticky Thinking	• Contributions by the 'boss'	• Agenda-less meetings
		• Meetings without strong chairing
	• Conversational use of imagery, stories or emotionally-charged descriptions	• Meetings that are known to run over time
	• Rehearsal of what's 'in vogue' in the organization	• Brainstorming or problem solving sessions that are not well structured

focus, purpose, or discipline, Sticky Thinking is more likely to occur. In addition to this, specific behaviors can invoke the habit such as the views expressed by the 'boss', the use in conversation of powerful language and imagery, and in instances where participants rehearse what is in fashion in the organizations. All else being equal, conversation and thinking will stick, at least for a while, to these actions.

What is interesting here is that so much of this happens more or less by accident. In many situations, the 'boss' may not want to extend undue influence over the discussion (although, of course, sometimes they will). In the field of leadership development, the phrase 'leaders cast long shadows' is commonly used to bring to the attention of leaders the point that each and every one of their actions becomes magnified far more than they imagine. I was told a story by an excellent organizational trouble-shooter and leadership teacher called Dr Mee-Yan Cheung Judge, who had made this same point with the Chief Executive Officer of a large successful company. The Chief Executive Officer wasn't 100 per cent convinced so Mee-Yan invited him to take part in an experiment, which for the next week he was invited to visibly carry around the building and into meetings a journal not usually associated with the business. For the sake of argument let us say it was *Fast Company* magazine. The instructions were not to refer to, or say anything about the magazine, but to see what influence this might have on staff. At the end of the month in which the experiment took place, the number of subscriptions taken up for the magazine was examined. They had gone up from six subscriptions to 80 and this is without the Chief Executive Officer saying a single word about the journal.

In reference to the sticky quality of imagery, stories or emotionally charged descriptions, no setting better illustrates this than a leadership development program. One of the senior leadership programs that I ran was a residential, four-week activity that attracted, on each run, something in the region of eight to ten visiting chief executive officer speakers, six to eight academic contributions from experts from business schools including London Business School and INSEAD, numerous topic-specific trainers and coaches, hundreds of interviews with staff from live case study organizations, high profile figures in politics, the media, the Armed Forces and the sporting world and with formal contributions from all of the participants. During the four-week program we would typically see something in the region of 250 people having an explicit space on the program to deliver a message.

I have absolutely no doubt that a relatively small number of 'sticky' presentations by these contributors directed the flows of discussion and thinking during the course of the month. What made these presentations so sticky was not necessarily the depth of content but was the way in which visual imagery, stories, or an emotional connection was made that seemed to imprint itself on the minds of the participants. I have seen this happen month after month and year after year to the point that now, whenever I select particularly 'sticky' contributions and contributors to a learning activity, I do so because I believe the trajectory of that contribution is where I want to take the group. By contrast, I have just as often seen people assembling conferences and looking for a 'motivating' or 'innovative' speaker to liven things up, without the slightest appreciation of where, through the stickiness of the presentations, this will lead the group and whether this is where the group need to be.

As leaders in an organization or anyone in a position to steer thinking in conversation, it is important to understand how the habit of Sticky Thinking can be implicitly endorsed simply through adopting a 'laissez-faire' attitude. Where the group doesn't have, as its purpose, to get things done, this is not a problem. So that with a group of friends chatting together, the joy of slipping from one topic to another without an endgame in mind is fine, and probably makes the discussion more entertaining. But where things need to be achieved it is important to remember that different forms of behavior carry different degrees of stickiness. The question to ask of yourself in any setting is, can I see this happening? What might I be doing to help this be understood as a behavioral 'norm'? And am I doing anything to help kick the habit?

In Table 1.6, I have outlined some of the other factors that can give rise to different thinking styles. These are not exhaustive but give a flavor of how habits are called upon and evidenced as 'right' through repeated use. I have focused, in particular, at the micro level on the specific language and type of questions that are used. It is in the act of conversation, in the act of turn taking, that so many habits are created.

First of all, if we focus for a moment at the micro level, we can see exactly how the 'sale' and adoption of thinking works and how thinking styles become habits. Without being fully aware of what we are doing, we offer up, in the course of conversations, different thinking styles to be taken by the recipient(s) of our utterances. So for example, if I hand a document to you and invite you to 'give me your analysis' of it, it opens up at a very fundamental level a tacit expectation that

Table 1.6 An illustration of the factors that trigger the deployment of different thinking styles

Thinking Style	Trigger questions	Language triggers	Environment triggers
Deficit Thinking	What do you think of this?	'Weaknesses', 'problems', 'deficiencies', 'shortfalls', 'risks', 'concerns', 'faults', 'but', 'however'	Encouragement rarely needed
Rational Thinking	What would be your analysis of this?	'Diagnosis', 'assessment', 'analysis', 'evaluation', 'reason', 'logic'	'Serious' business meeting conditions
Common Sense Thinking	What is our view on this?	'Sensible', 'reasonable', 'on balance', 'straw poll', 'all things considered'	Gathering of 'generalists'
Binary Thinking	What are the options here?	'Either, or', 'change tack', 'on the one hand'	Crisis situations
Equity Thinking	Are we being consistent here?	'Fair', 'unfair', 'equitable', 'equal', 'consistent', 'comparable'	Gathering of representatives of a larger grouping e.g. union representative

(a) you will respond and (b) that the language that I have used will steer your response. In the example given, the use of the term 'analysis' is likely to cause you to think, within the blinking of an eye, what form of response would fit with the language used. You would probably associate the word 'analysis' with all that is encapsulated in Rational Thinking, that is the use of logical reasoning, a search for sequences, for associations and for causality, consideration of evidence, and all against a model of 'reasonableness'. You would not think this is 'one of those occasions' where I am being asked about my feelings. The use of language at every turn of the conversation serves to prime other participants for the thinking style they should take.

This does not mean that it is a foregone conclusion that the expected style will be adopted, but because our habits of thinking operate at a level usually well below the radar, we rarely pause to question or challenge the terms in which the utterance is framed. For example, if I say to you 'are we being consistent here?' you are unlikely to contest whether consistency, or ultimately fairness, is an acceptable mode of thinking to adopt. You are more likely, due to the sticky quality of questions, to find yourself searching for similar instances of the matter examined to discover examples of inconsistency. There are other reasons too why you are unlikely to challenge the way an utterance is framed and the thinking style it tacitly evokes:

- Thinking styles are rarely noticed and are difficult to challenge as a result
- It can be seen as churlish to contest something so seemingly mundane and neutral
- It breaks the flow of conversation, and in group settings this leaves participants unclear as to how to act next. The awkwardness that can often follow causes participants to round on the perpetrator of the conversational break and bring them back into line

The way we tacitly accept thinking styles is similar to many other forms of social behavior. An unremarkable and routine illustration of this is the social act of greeting one another. When we hear the question 'how are you?' we immediately understand, in the first instance, that we are required to respond. Secondly, we understand that our response should not be to literally provide a debrief of how we are feeling, rather we should recognize the question as a convenient way of making polite contact and a signal that we should say something like 'fine thanks, and you?' Importantly though, it is the first question that determines the trajectory of the next stage of the interaction. As with the previous example of the Equity Thinking question 'are we being consistent here?' once the trajectory is set it normally continues until its course is run.

Let us take from Table 1.6 another example of the question 'what do you think of this?' and imagine that the focus of the question is, say, a new design for a flatter organizational structure provided by a task force reporting to the top team. The top team will hear the words 'what do you think of this?' but will hear the invitation 'can you find anything wrong with this?' We know this is what they will really hear because as they politely hunt down, one by one, all of the problems, flaws, and weaknesses in the report, the task force won't once indicate that their response is out of place. They might look thoroughly demoralized but you won't hear them saying 'that's not what we meant' or 'why are you focusing on the deficiencies?' Furthermore, once the first question has set the trajectory of the response, the theme of faults and shortcomings will be on the agenda, and the long trajectory of the deficit conversation will begin. Set your alarm for an hour later and you might just see the deficit path come to an end. Like an athlete being handed a baton in an Olympic relay, you won't see them stopping to complain that the baton is too heavy or awkward to hold, they will just take it and run and pretty soon hand it on to the next runner who will do the same.

Our thinking habits are shared in conversation and repeated until they are neither noticed nor questioned. This starts at a very early stage in our lives and, by the time we reach adulthood and put them to use in organizational settings, they become like the baton in a relay race.

As managers and leaders of organizations we need to pause for a moment to consider our own role in this. What do we do that shapes the habits of our staff? What paths are we inviting our staff to travel down? And, in conversation, can we consciously make use of thinking habits to shift the thinking of others and to bring about change?

2 Switching Controls to Manual

Board meetings on the beach

Beach holidays can be wonderful things. Imagine it, you're lying there with your back sinking into the coral sand, the sky lit up and expanding across the horizon and the sea rhythmically pattering up the shore and then sliding back into the ocean. You take a deep breath and let it out for what seems like a lifetime. Time slows down and it's as if your mind is hovering high in the warm thermals above you. The world is a million miles away. But for a moment your thinking drifts into a problem; a difficulty at work; a snag in a relationship; a complicated decision you need to take. And as you retrieve the problem from your memory and begin to re-constitute it, you notice something is different. It's the same difficult problem but somehow, as you lie there, it has taken new shape. What you experienced previously as tenseness, a tightening in the chest, there is now a feeling of openness, of possibility. Before, where options appeared limited, now magically, they seem abundant. And as well as more choices seeming available to you, you see different ways of tackling the problem; approaches and solutions that are in every way untypical for you; solutions that you imagine other people finding, certainly not you. In short, as you lie there doing nothing, problems that previously seemed intractable have opened up like an oyster washed onto the shore, and the answers are there for the taking.

The solution to our thinking challenges can't be met by holding board meetings on the beach, as attractive as it may sound. The serious point here is that certain conditions will unleash a broader range of responses to existing problems. The prize lies in finding the way to do this that can, unlike our beach holiday example, be introduced into our daily lives easily, seamlessly, and without fuss. Tricks and one-off gimmicks won't do the job. Breaking out to apply the 'x' technique or to apply a trademark method will not do it. These methods can be good particularly if well facilitated, but the easiest way to recover the benefits of new ways of thinking is to make them a part of how we are – to make use of, and work with, our habit-making behavior and simply add a few more powerful habits in to the pot.

In Chapter 1 of this book I have highlighted two important features of the way we attack problems. The first is our tendency to automatically drop our response to any problem into a channel of thinking, such as Deficit Thinking, which pre-determines and narrows where the analysis will take us. The second feature of our thinking is that it is located and steered in conversation; conversation usually with others, but also conversations we have with ourselves as we reflect and privately work through issues. Both of these features provide us with important clues as to how we might broaden our repertoire of thinking habits and help shape the thinking of others. For most of this chapter I will focus on this question.

Put thinking habits on your radar

The thinking habits that we adopt on a daily basis have become so routine that we no longer notice them. Getting them back onto the radar becomes our first priority if we are to remember what they are there to do and where they will lead us.

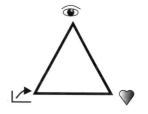

One of our new habits should be to incorporate three simple actions every time we engage in thinking either alone or in social settings.

The first step should be to monitor and look for the thinking channel that is in use (the eye at the top of the triangle). It will typically be one of the channels explored in Chapter 1 and shown in Table 2.1. You may, of course, spot other less common thinking channels and it will be of benefit to familiarize yourself with when and how these are used. Of course, people will switch from channel to channel and there is no guarantee of the length of time that will

Table 2.1 Common thinking channels

- Deficit Thinking
- Rational Thinking
- Common Sense Thinking
- Sticky Thinking
- Equity Thinking
- Binary Thinking

typically be spent in each channel. Nevertheless, of what you can be sure is that, where discussions involve two or more people, thinking channels will provide a form of unseen agenda or pathway for the discussion. Vigilance is required therefore so that you can both keep an eye on what is happening while also contributing, as you would do in the normal course of events.

The second step should be to consider the trajectory that each thinking channel will take (the chart at the bottom left of the triangle). For example, Rational Thinking tends to steer a course toward a logical and sometimes mechanistic analysis of the data and options available, and away from feelings, emotions, and human factors. Knowing where Rational Thinking will take you, for example, is important. Woody Allen once said that he wasn't worried about advanced civilizations landing on earth and taking us over because they were centuries ahead of us. Rather, what worried him the most was being invaded by aliens who would be only fifteen minutes ahead; they would always get a parking space and they would always be first in the queue for the movies. The same principle applies here; seeing and understanding the trajectory of thinking channels buys you time and prepares you for the movement of thinking in conversation. Most people do not typically do this, even those chairing or leading discussions.

The third step and final habit to adopt at this stage should be to periodically assess, almost like radar sweeping its territory, how people are feeling during the thinking process (the heart at the bottom right of the triangle). This includes you; in fact, you may be the best source of data on the feelings of those participating. In particular here you are looking to assess:

- Energy levels (high–low)
- Emotional connection to the issue explored (engagement–disengagement)
- Emotional lows and highs (boredom–excitement)

This is very important, and later on in this chapter I will illustrate in a little more detail how this contributes to the conversion of thinking into action.

You will need skill to be mindful of the three points of the triangle so that, at the same time, you can both be inside the conversation as an active participant, and outside as an observer monitoring what is going on. By far the strongest force will be to pull you into the conversation and, without doubt, if you see a deficiency in an argument or an inconsistency you may find yourself wading in knee deep into the Deficit

Thinking or Equity Thinking channel. Once you are there it is often too late because you will have set the pathway for others to follow.

If we look to the field of social research and the methodological traditions associated with it, we can borrow from one methodological framework that highlights the differences between simultaneous observation and participation as a means of studying the social world. Below are four typologies that characterize diffcrent approaches to social research:

- *Complete participant*: the researcher employing this role attempts to engage fully in the activities of the group or organization under investigation. Their role is covert (hidden) and the intentions of the researcher are not made explicit. From a data-gathering perspective it is recognized that this approach can take the researcher to areas that are not usually accessible. The information gathered may not be available by any other means. This carries the risk of 'going native', losing objectivity, and becoming too embedded in the subject examined to see it sufficiently clearly. The tacit communication to the group is 'I am one of you'.
- *Participant as observer*: the researcher adopts an overt (open) role and makes their presence and intentions known to the group. Participation is still the defining feature of the 'seen' contribution of the researcher, although the group understands that the researcher has dual intentions (to participate and to observe). Traditional concerns about the risk of 'going native' or losing objectivity are still present although less significant than with the complete participant role. The key advantage is that the researcher is able to gather more natural and authentic data without having to cover their tracks or remain in the field for extended periods of time. The tacit communication to the group is 'I want to understand you by doing what you do'.
- *Observer as participant*: the researcher moves away from the idea of full participation. The research method will involve site visits, interviews, observation of naturally occurring events, and social gatherings. The observation process is more formal and, to a limited extent, the researcher may participate in what they see occurring. It is an approach that has some elements of objectivity in that the researcher has little influence over what happens. Here, though, there may be a risk of misunderstanding as a consequence of the distance between the observer and the subject. The tacit communication to the group is 'I am foremost a researcher but I wish to taste a little of the lives you lead'.
- *Complete observer*: the researcher is uninvolved and detached from the subject matter and passively records behavior at a distance, such

as a researcher sitting in a classroom, making observations of pupils and their teacher. There is no contact between researcher and subject and this provides a level of 'scientific objectivity'. One of the risks is that there is a limit to how deeply the researcher can understand what is going on, particularly as they do not benefit from the experience of 'doing'. The tacit communication to the group is 'I will watch you from a distance'.

What we can borrow from here are the relevant principles of the participant as observer role. Whether you are a senior executive in an organization, a leader, a chair, or anyone engaged in steering thinking behavior, you are first and foremost an active player in the world you inhabit. But you also need to be an observer of the thinking process as thinking channels are adopted, as the trajectory is followed and this affects the way people feel about what is happening.

People in senior positions need to pay particular attention to this not least because they 'cast very long shadows' and can have a disproportionate influence on how an issue is explored. The modeling effect that leaders have is striking, and at times they may need to shift down a notch from the 'participant as observer' role to the 'observer as participant' position to see more clearly how the thinking is developing.

Prepare the way for transformational thinking

In the context of conducting a conversation – a social thinking process – there are three more features of the new habit that will help to position us well for much better thinking.

Fight the compulsion to fill the space

If you have the time to observe people talking, and if you screen out the content of what they say, you will notice some predictable patterns about the way we interact with one another. As outlined earlier, one way in which we engage with one another is in a turn-taking fashion. I say something, you respond. You say something, I respond. It is like playing tennis that goes on for game after game in the hot sun. In conversation even if one person takes up more airtime than another, the tacit understanding is that it is normal to take turns. When this social norm is broken, for example, if I offer a view on a movie I have just watched and you choose not to respond,

I will either assume that you didn't hear me, or that there is meaning in your decision not to respond. Perhaps you are annoyed with me, or there is something else more important on your mind. Whatever the variations, the underlying 'rule' is that once someone has finished speaking, it is expected that someone else will fill the gap. This can cause problems for us if we wish to break away from an existing thinking channel but have perhaps less than a second to find a new path. In the same vein, once I am speaking and knee deep in mud in the trenches, it's difficult to take a helicopter view of the battlefield.

In business settings, where to stay silent may imply a lack of certainty or ability, the pressure to say something, to say anything, no matter how off-target or inappropriate is great. Observing who quickly fills the conversational gaps in meetings, for example, will usually help you to identify your extroverts who, after doing so, often kick themselves for 'talking so much garbage'. The introverts of course kick themselves after the meeting when they find the perfect response but about an hour too late. Either way, airtime is something for which we typically scramble and find ourselves compelled to fill.

The Eastern practice of meditation provides a wonderful illustration of how difficult it is to simply put thoughts aside for a moment. The following extracts are taken from first hand accounts of some of the barriers that are thrown up as people, usually Westerners, attempt to meditate

Meditation is hard. I can't, for the life of me, clear my mind. So much comes swimming through. When I am able to quiet my mind I fall asleep, a nice deep sleep but still it is sleeping and not meditating. Is there any music I should listen to? I know it should be quiet time but maybe some drums would help me. Author unknown (appeared on blog chatroom, 3 May 2005)

Most meditation works by focusing on an object of concentration; the breath entering and leaving the body in this case. We generally meditate for 30 minutes at a time. It is very hard to concentrate on just one thing, and when I first began to meditate I found my mind constantly bringing up other things for me to think about. Slowly, over a period of months of practice, one can learn to let the distractions of the mind drift away, enabling one to concentrate more on what one is doing. I have made some progress, and now am able to meditate for about 10–20 seconds without any distractions. Author unknown (commenting on meditation technique called Samatha, Internet).

The message that we should take from these examples in relation to meditation, and from our own experiences in daily life and business settings, is that as we engage in social thinking we must escape from our own compulsion to react. In essence, we must routinely introduce a break into the flow of conversation and, where needed, re-set the pattern. As we are aware, this is not easy to do; and it doesn't mean we have to resort to imposing an awkward silence. However, we do need to bring some tranquility to our own mind and begin to replace reacting with thinking.

Put conversations in a holding pattern

London's Heathrow airport is the third busiest airport in the world, closely behind Chicago's O'Hare and Atlanta's Hartsfield. Because it is such a significant international hub, it has the highest flow-through of international passengers in the world. Each year, there are approximately 500,000 take-offs and landings escorting almost 65 million passengers to their destinations, enough passengers to cover the entire populations of New York, London, Paris, Beijing, Delhi, and Tokyo with room to spare. While it may be disappointing therefore for passengers to hear from the PA system as they come into land at Heathrow: 'We do not yet have clearance to land at Heathrow and Air Traffic Control have placed us in a holding pattern' it is an entirely understandable response to the level of traffic that needs to be handled safely. When we bear in mind too that in any one hour there will be around 60 take-offs or landings, the wait of five to ten minutes doesn't seem so bad after all. The time it takes to get though passport control is enough to bring a man to his knees, but that's another story. In the spirit of this point I would like you, for a moment, to put this thought on hold and reflect upon it as you read the next paragraph.

For years I have been interested in the contribution that the social sciences can make in comparison with the natural sciences. I was brought up in a very pragmatic family; one that, in social science parlance, is very 'positivist'. Academic theory was viewed as somewhat indulgent at best and a sign of weakness at worst. In my family, the world was often one of black and white, of common sense or nonsense, and of utility or uselessness. Understandably influenced, although not holding the same perspective, I have studied in various forms the ways in which sociology, social psychology, ethnomethodology and all the 'soft' 'ologies' can be connected with everyday life.

One of the most fundamental differences that social scientists have drawn between the locus of study in the two fields is well described by the phenomenological philosopher Alfred Schutz:

> The world of nature, as explored by the natural scientist, does not 'mean' anything to molecules, atoms and electrons. But the observational field of the social scientist – social reality – has a specific meaning and relevance structure for the human beings living, acting and thinking within it. (p. 59)

Please now turn your mind back to our airport scenario. The comment that Schutz makes is relevant to the practice adopted by airports across the world that direct air traffic into holding patterns. What is distinctive about the sociological study of the world as compared to the natural sciences is that in the social world the subjects of examination and the people who constitute the 'observational field' are capable of making sense of what they experience and altering their thinking and actions accordingly. The 'molecules, atoms, and electrons' that constitute the matter examined in the natural sciences do not alter their behavior other than in entirely predictable and reactive ways triggered by forces and elements around them.

The holding pattern principle should therefore be thought of as the space between reaction and thoughtful action – a space that is encroached upon by everyday distractions, by thinking channels in use, by the norms of turn-taking in social interaction and by the pressure to do something, anything, however uninformed. Holding this space open, as you were instructed to do in reading these paragraphs, can be difficult, but enables us to make better sense of what is happening and to allow a thoughtful response.

The first step in preparing the way therefore is to fight the compulsion to fill the conversational space. The second is to put the thinking process in a holding pattern to buy time and, in doing so, to put aside some 'headspace' to consider what should happen next. What this might mean in practice is an extra few minutes or even a few seconds – just long enough to avoid being forced to react. Methods of doing this vary and will need to be matched to the style of the individual.

By way of illustration, imagine a situation where a meeting is taking place between three or four senior managers who have got together to explore the possibility, say, of forming a strategic partnership with a key competitor. Some of the thinking has already been done about how this might happen and one of the company's directors, Ray, who is taking the lead on this, has set up a meeting with colleagues to talk further. The discussion has got off the ground quickly and within a few minutes the lead director is already working through the potential difficulties he sees with the proposal (Deficit Thinking channel). You have resisted the temptation to join in and although you too can see many more problems and risks and would love to add them in, if only to unburden yourself, you sagely hold back. You recognize the need to put the conversation into a holding pattern to give you and the other colleagues time to steer the conversation and the thinking process purposefully toward more fertile ground. Some of the options that you might have at your disposal are:

- Seek further descriptive (not analytical) elaboration from the problem holder/presenter: '*Ray, it would be really helpful to have a little more background to this proposal. Do you think you could describe how we got to this position?*'
- Invite the problem holder/presenter to outline what they hope to achieve by the end of the encounter: '*Ray, it would be really helpful to me if you could tell me what would be a useful outcome to this discussion.*'
- Provide a neutral conversational distraction and keep it going for as long as you need: '*One thing that occurs to me is that it is interesting how so many of our competitors now see us as a potential partner*', '*you must have been working at this for some time now*', etc.
- Introduce a physical break to the conversation: '*Perhaps we could take a break for a couple of minutes*', '*can I get anyone a coffee?*' '*would you mind if we captured some of this on a flipchart?*'
- Explicitly recognize the need to select a process for the discussion: '*I think it would be really useful for us to stand back for a moment and think about how best to work through this*', '*how can we work together on this so that Ray gets full value from the meeting?*'

The effect of any of these interventions will be to create stillness in the thinking process and to communicate to those participating that sometimes going slower can get us to our destination more quickly.

Create the right environment

The environment in which people come together to think is critical to the quality of thinking that takes place. In the natural world, we can see ever more clearly the impact that weather patterns, urban expansion, farming methods, industrialization, and migration can have on the world in which we live. The learning we draw from this is the need to see more clearly the relationship between ostensibly unconnected natural conditions in the environment and the subject under study.

There is a well-known story concerning the reign of Mao Tse-Tung, which helps to illustrate this theme of interdependence. The Chinese writer Ningkun Wu who was incarcerated for 22 years in China and served in a forced labor camp as a counterrevolutionary wrote his memoirs under the title *A Single Tear*. In his book, one of the accounts he gave of his time in China highlighted the ever-extending power of Chairman Mao. *In 1958,* Chairman Mao Tse-Tung was keen, in addition to seeing his political will exercised, to extend control over the forces of nature. To this end, he launched what he called 'A Campaign Against Four Evils' in which Chairman Mao inspired the Chinese people to help stamp out the 'evils' of rats, flies, mosquitoes, and sparrows. Mao was particularly driven to single out sparrows as they were responsible for the theft of millions of tons of food and grain each year from the Chinese people.

On one legendary day, as the story goes, the Chinese people carried out the will of Chairman Mao and reeked havoc on the sparrow population. They were known to bang pots loudly, to chase sparrows out of bushes and trees, to do everything in their power to relentlessly reduce the sparrow population. The poor birds were hunted down and driven to a state of exhaustion. The next day official newspapers reported that millions of sparrows had successfully been eradicated and fried sparrows had been eaten across China.

However, as successful as the operation had been, during the course of the next two years China experienced unprecedented crop loss and consequently, famine. The principal cause had been an enormous growth in wheat-eating insects that, under normal conditions, would have been eaten themselves by the bird, and particularly the sparrow, population. The interventions of leaders can sometimes be a terrible thing.

The focus of our gaze, whatever we are studying, needs to be both on the object of our interest and on the context or system in which that object exists. Another illustration of this is the much bigger dilemma we face in relation to the horrifyingly rapid extinction of swathes of species of plants and animals. Called by some as the 'sixth mass extinction', the data that have been accumulated by scientists over decades of study leave us in no doubt that environmental factors are leading to the demise of some of our most aged species.

Six large sets of data collected over the past ... 40 years in England, Wales and Scotland were analyzed by Jeremy Thomas of the Natural Environment Research Council ... More than 20,000 volunteers submitted over 15 million records of species ... [showing] that 71% of butterfly species have decreased over the last 20 years and 56% of birds and 28% of plants ... **the current extinction is being precipitated by the widespread loss of habitats because of human activity**. (*New Scientist*, 18 March 2004)

Scientists say there have been five mass extinctions in history, they contend we're on the verge of another one, and humankind is mostly to blame ... Experts say the threat to plant and animal species threatens our own survival, since man and nature are dependent on each other. And the key to saving endangered species is saving the world's forests ... **But civilization needs trees for lumber, pulp and fuel. Global consumption of wood and paper continues to rise ... The problem is, as the forest area begins to decrease and reach critically low levels, environmental processes begin to collapse, soil erosion begins to increase, the amount of species that inhabit the forest begin to disappear, the productivity of land begins to decrease**. (CNN broadcast, 2 January 2000)

In many ways we now understand, in part thanks to the spotlight provided by environmentalists and the work of the scientific community, how in the natural world living species are being eradicated by factors external to them – factors in the environment. In business, however, and specifically in the business of thinking, we have some catching up to do.

Getting back to the subject of the conditions for success in business thinking I want to recap on where we are with the main steps outlined in this part. I have set out the need, in any thinking process, to do the following:

1. to monitor the use of thinking channels in conversation, their trajectory and how people feel – to do this routinely and regularly
2. to fight the compulsion to fill conversational thinking space – to do this routinely and regularly
3. to periodically put thinking conversations in a holding pattern to hold off the urge to react and to divert more time into thinking – to do this routinely and regularly
4. to foster the right environment – one that will help grow high-quality thinking

Creating the right environment for social thinking needs to take into account the important distinction between the natural and the social world. As we discussed earlier, people in the social world strive to make sense of what is going on (unlike atoms, electrons, etc. which react in complex but predictable ways). The social arena calls upon us to constantly navigate our way through power structures, group and organizational norms, role boundaries, social relationships, differential attitudes to responsibility, ownership and accountability, proving one's worth and the competitive forces at play.

The environment in which we conduct our social thinking needs, where it can, to quieten the white noise that these factors usually create. Picture yourself in front of one of those hi-fi graphic equalizers so popular in the 1980s, and imagine turning down the volume on the internal voices that inevitably speak to you about role, about power, about the right (or not) to speak, and about the pressure to perform. Once you have begun down this path it becomes a habit that is easy to keep. In the early stages it requires an active internal dialogue but as time passes you will, more and more, put these thoughts to the background. This is the first step in creating the right environment.

This, however, is not enough. The thinking environment needs more than just an absence (or quietening) of unhelpful distractions. Your graphic equalizer needs to emphasize and turn up the volume on the other areas so that the thinking environment feels like the one outlined in Table 2.2.

These are important for the following reasons:

- 'Purpose' helps combat the Sticky Thinking tendency that will always cause thinking to wander off course.
- 'Valuing time' is the 'belt and braces' solution we need to stay on-target with the purpose and the discipline needed to do this well.
- 'Honesty and authenticity' are the ways we attack over-used thinking patterns that have become a habit for habit's sake.
- The spirit of 'group exploration' is our strongest arrow in the quiver. The sense of joint responsibility and exploration coupled

Table 2.2 Four features of a high quality social thinking environment

- One with purpose (in the sense that thinking is a job to be done)
- One where time is valuable and valued
- One where honesty and authenticity is non-negotiable, and;
- One where thinking is conducted as if it were a group exploration

with the requirement of a clear purpose drives the best thinking to the surface. It does so by avoiding jealousies or competition or without invoking the less useful attributes of role or power. It allows experimentation and playfulness by framing the experience as an exploration. It also builds in learning as a core component of the thinking process.

Creating an environment that quietens less desirable intrusions and accentuates the four qualities in Table 2.2 is a pragmatic issue of what works in different settings and for different people. The philosophy that I adopt is that the most successful and enduring strategies for achieving behavioral change are those strategies that are incorporated as seamlessly as possible within existing 'tracks' of behavior. With this in mind, you may wish to pick from the list below those strategies that could most easily be turned into habits in your environment/ culture:

- Use a purpose-led agenda (rather than an action or issue led agenda).
- Establish ground rules at the outset of each thinking process (to outline or elaborate on the four environmental conditions above).
- Use a confidentiality device (such as Chatham House Rules[1]) to signal the importance of honesty and realness.
- Explicitly name the mode of the thinking process as an enquiry or exploration.
- Denote the thinking process as something that stands outside of the normal lines of reporting and accountability.
- Denote the thinking process as an action-learning activity.[2]
- Make use of a process facilitator who can attend to issues of ground rules, timing, and helping a group move toward its purpose.

Another critical factor in helping to nurture and sustain the right environment is the modeling behavior adopted by senior people. This is meant both in the context of thinking conversations and also more generally as senior people go about their daily business in the organization. Such modeling behavior provides, above all, the permission for staff to conduct themselves in particular ways. Permission is meant in a positive sense and not to characterize staff in more junior positions as child like.

As people make sense of their environment, for example within a work setting, they quickly reach an understanding of what is allowed and what is not. Like all thinking habits, this has the benefit of making the consumption of our own effort efficient. In doing so we adopt the line of least resistance so as to channel our energies in fruitful directions. After time though our understanding of the boundaries delineating what is permitted from what isn't become hardened and the possibility of behaving outside and beyond the perimeter becomes less and less likely. Much of the work leaders need to do involves getting into the heads of their staff to understand where they set the boundaries and, where needed, to help them to re-shape their own sense of possibility. The quickest way to do this is to show that acting outside of the perimeter is fine, and it occurs without punishment or retribution, or in practice, without a loaded look of consternation on the face of senior executives.

In practice, this means that senior figures in organizations should act as if they too enjoy exploring and enquiring *alongside* colleagues as if (which of course they should) they share a common purpose. It means that senior figures should act as if they cherish the time they have with staff; they should show their appreciation for the energy that people invest and visibly learn from others. It means that senior figures should behave authentically, and signal that progress can only be made through honest conversation. It means that senior figures might also establish ground rules for meetings or use facilitators to discuss important issues. All of these behaviors help to grow and nurture an environment that supports high-quality thinking.

Finally, we can look to the physical design of buildings and, in particular, discussion spaces to foster an environment that reflects, among others, the principles outlined in Table 2.2. In Kansas City, North America, Chuck Dymer, an excellent teacher and trainer in the field of creativity, and Master Trainer of Edward de Bono's thinking methods, has devoted his energies to building a space that accelerates the thinking process.

The area, called the 'The Idea Loft', is based around principles of achieving a common purpose, of facilitating free movement between ideas, of using time with care and creating a spirit of discovery and exploration. This is done, as the pictures illustrate, through the deliberate use of large empty spaces contrasted with cozy, homely spaces; through giant focus boards that remind participants of where their attention should be; through the use of wall-projected timers and through relaxation areas that foster an attitude of openness and honesty. The Idea Loft even has its own chef. Chuck Dymer, President of PeopleWorks Inc., explains what led him to create this environment.

For years I've been helping organizations generate ideas and new products. I noticed a long time ago that space matters. Diverse locations affect thinking; a tennis club in London; a Victorian fortress and a dude ranch come to mind. But these [settings] weren't designed to enhance business strategies. I have been through what every business person has too – boring meetings, stale hotels and conference rooms not fit for man nor beast. That's why I designed The Idea Loft.

The question you may want to ask of yourself is, if in conducting your discussions and meetings, would an environment like this help or hinder the process? If the answer is help rather than hinder there will be aspects of the physical environment that you too can replicate wherever you are.

Trigger the right thinking channel

We are now armed with an appreciation of the need to monitor the use of thinking habits in action; in particular to be mindful of where thinking channels will take us and how they make us feel. In thinking conversations, we understand the importance of holding back when the urge to react takes over, of deliberately taking the opportunity to keep the conversation up in the air to buy thinking time, and the need to foster an environment where high quality thinking can thrive. Now I would like you to imagine that, having made these a habit of yours, you can give your attention to setting up the thinking channels that will take thinking conversations forward. This is where you, in the words you use and the way you talk, can directly sway thinking and set a pattern that will do its own work for you. The four actions that follow are those that will have the greatest impact in the moment of thinking. Explained in more detail in the following paragraphs, I have called these:

- Act in the present, live in the future
- Mind your language
- Set your thoughts on fire, and
- Keep on the move

Act in the present, live in the future

If we think about the notion of time as being divisible into three categories of past, present, and future, you will have noticed that much of what I have said so far has been to encourage a shift in attention from the past toward the future. For example, the trap of being 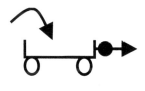 compelled to react in thinking conversations ties us to the past; our actions being framed by what has just been said. My proposal that we should periodically put conversations into holding patterns is there so that we can focus on what happens next rather than what has just occurred. Creating the right environment is entirely about the future; about what will create sustainable conditions for high quality thinking.

The Armed Forces use the phrase 'the fog of war' to recognize that conflict situations are loaded with uncertainty and only a limited number of eventualities can be planned for. Embedded in each operation will be different levels of mission so that if things go off course, as the fog descends, and the lowest level of mission (the most specific) becomes unachievable, each soldier will be able to refer to the next most relevant level up from which to draw their instructions.

Action in the present is shaped by a desired state in the future. The future acts as a magnet for the present and in this example it also provides flexibility and local freedom to get there.

With our thinking interventions in conversation, we need too to orientate ourselves to the future. We need to intervene in a way that sets up a pathway that will lead the conversation to fulfilling its purpose. We need, in a way, to view our contribution as a gift rather than an opportunity to get something for ourselves – to prove our worth, to score points, to form alliances, or to win. As senior players within the organization the switch in thinking needs to be away from 'what can I get here now to help me meet a need?' to 'what can I give here now to help us move toward our destination?'

A classic coaching intervention provides a very good demonstration of how, in thinking conversations, this movement toward the future can be achieved. A well-used coaching question is 'what would need to happen in order for you to feel that your goal (whatever it may be) had been achieved?' The question compels the coachee to mentally envisage where they need to be and to begin the thinking work on how to get there. It picks the coachee up from the past and gets them walking to the future. Let us explore more ways in which the framing of questions and words we use help this progression toward a future state.

Mind your language

In October 1998, General Augusto Pinochet, the former President of Chile, was arrested at the London Bridge hospital in England on a warrant that alleged that between 1973 and 1983 he committed atrocities against Spanish citizens. Although not part of the initial investigation, it was also put that Pinochet 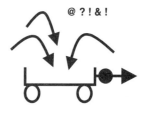 was responsible for widespread torture, 3,000 'disappearances', and scores of brutal interrogations during his 17-year dictatorship. At the time, the Government of Chile officially opposed the warrant and put the case that Pinochet was under no obligation to testify. Feelings were polarized among the Chilean people who, in some quarters demonstrated violently on the streets against the decision taken by the UK government, while others rejoiced to see Pinochet finally brought to justice.

Very shortly afterwards, and during the time when Pinochet was still held under house arrest in London, I co-delivered some training in Santiago, Chile on behalf of the British Government and by invitation of the Chilean government. The program had been planned quite some months in advance and, in spite of the circumstances, it was finally decided that the program should progress as planned. The purpose was to share, together with the Chilean Civil Service, the reforms that were underway in the UK and how these had been advanced and focused. On the very day that I arrived, as I was being taken with a colleague to the conference center, I learned from the driver of the government car that during the previous week an explosive device had been removed from the underside of the chassis. I thought things couldn't get any more worrying until we arrived at the training venue only to learn that it was the headquarters of the Chilean military, the same military of which General Pinochet, that's right, 'General' Pinochet, was the head.

The first few hours were an unnerving time as not only were all our coffee breaks shared with numerous people in full military regalia, but within minutes of arriving at the center, the group of almost a hundred Chilean officials participating in the program, had broken out into all six verses of the Chilean national anthem. I imagine that even from the back of the hall the heavy bead of sweat trickling down my cheek would have been visible.

As the week progressed, I got to spend time with the participants and I began to settle in. Things weren't as they might have appeared from the outset and by the end of the week I had made some wonderful friends and I developed a real love for the country and its people. I have since visited the country on a number of occasions. During the course of the week my colleague and I found ourselves relying more and more heavily on the two interpreters that simultaneously translated everything we said. For much of the time, when in formal sessions, the focus of our teaching was on the way that in the UK we worked alongside and held interviews with stakeholders, taxpayers, and other officials to understand their needs. I found myself using the word 'interview' an awful lot throughout the week as it helped to capture the formal and collaborative nature of many of the government reforms that we discussed. It was only at the end of the program that an excellent Chilean patriot, and our host for the week, devilishly informed me that the interpreters, quite honorably but unfortunately incorrectly, had been translating the word 'interview' into the word 'interrogation'. When I had been told this I thought I was going to faint as I frantically searched my memory for all the occasions I had sagely advised officials to interrogate their staff, their colleagues, and their citizens. Under these circumstances you can imagine the Chilean people thinking it was about time for some more reforms in the UK. One of the more serious points I want to highlight with this example is that words have extraordinary power in the way they steer thinking and the 'baggage' that they bring with them.

There is a well-known conundrum that you may have heard where a father and son have gone hunting and an accident occurs and the son is rushed to hospital. On arrival the boy is ushered into the operating theatre and the doctor declares 'I cannot operate on this boy. He is my son'. The conundrum is – who is the doctor? The answer of course is that the doctor is the son's mother; obvious once you know the answer, less so if you've heard it for the first time. This conundrum is sometimes used to illustrate that we can make sexist assumptions and, in this instance, that we don't automatically think of doctors as being female. I do not wish to debate this here, rather I want to pause for a moment on what causes us, in this story, to be led to this erroneous judgment. The way that this works is that, through the use of carefully chosen words such as 'hunting', 'father', 'son', 'rushed', and 'accident', a distinctly masculine picture is created. These words lead the mind into a male world so that when the question is asked – who is the doctor? We find it hard to make the mental leap that is required. We almost need a reverse gear to take our thinking out of the dead end into which we have been driven.

In the process of social thinking, one of the most powerful ways in which we can use words and phrasing to trigger different thinking responses is in the framing of questions. Constructing questions skillfully is an art form and holds the key to new habits of thinking. It is also perhaps the single most effective way we can significantly accelerate our thinking. If you take only one thing away from this book let it be this.

I want you to imagine a serious discussion being held between a handful of members of a work team. Let's suppose that they are sales team responsible for the launch of a new marketing campaign. They have been very successful over recent months and have won a lot of business. Unfortunately, as success breeds success, they have found themselves with too much work to do, given the size of the team. The boss won't sanction an increase in resources but expects the ever-increasing workload to be delivered to the same high standard, if not better. In various other forms, this happens all the time. The team assembles for an emergency meeting to solve the problem. The team leader opens with a few questions intended to steer the group to a solution. What might these typically be?

Q1. How can we get more done without taking on more staff?
Q2. What are the higher priority tasks on which we should focus?
Q3. Can anybody put in more hours?
Q4. Can anyone think of how we can work more quickly?

All of the questions listed above are by no means stupid or poor. They are a typical set of responses to the problem faced. Unfortunately, they do not trigger or direct the thinking in a helpful way. They are, in essence, a re-statement of the problem with a question mark placed at the end. You can almost picture the tumbleweeds being blown across the table as the group thinks of a response. What then would be the kind of questions that would breath life into this problem?

Q5. What are we doing right that is making us so successful at this work?
Q6. If we were able to crack this problem what might we be doing differently?
Q7. How would we cope if the work were to triple again next week?
Q8. How would we solve this and sell it as a solution to one of our clients?

Remember, too, the encouragement at the start of this chapter to monitor how people feel in 'thinking' conversations. In this scenario, using the first set of questions, you can imagine the sense of woe and despair the questions serve to evoke. At best, they provide some motion toward a solution. The second set of questions however has a feeling of possibility. They create a loosening-up of the situation and, as a result, release some energy into the conversation. Better still though; they re-frame the problem so that it can be accessed in an entirely different way. The first option (Q5) is an invitation to consider the strengths that the team possesses and to be curious about what might happen if those strengths were better leveraged. The third question (Q7) forces an examination of how to respond if things *really* were bad (in fact three times as bad). The benefit here is that, as the team works back from the crisis-solutions of the nightmare scenario to the current problem they bring with them a different range of possibilities from those it would typically have found.

Underpinning all of this is the certain belief that I hold that we already possess the solutions to our problems. It is just a matter of gaining access to them. Questions are perhaps the most powerful tool we have to find the way in.

Let's take another scenario. You are in a senior-level meeting to explore the kind of culture toward which the organization should be lead. The top team, of which you are a part, wants to explicitly develop a leadership agenda and to do so with a cultural destination in mind. You find yourself chairing the meeting and the responsibility falls to you to frame the first question that will direct the group's thinking. How do you begin? You probably start with some context about why the group is gathered. Maybe if you are keen to make it a success, you introduce some ground rules. Then the moment comes, what do you ask? Let's consider two options. The first is: 'Could I hear some ideas on the attitudes and behaviors we want to see displayed in this organization?' The second is: 'What are the attitudes and behaviors that would make us most proud and excited to work here?'

Neither one of these questions is neutral. The first may appear so, which is perhaps why it could be a common way to frame a question that is not unduly influential, allowing space for people to think, not appearing to offer an agenda without first agreeing it with the group etc. However, both lay down a pathway for the thinking to follow. The problem is that the track laid down by the first question is harder to see. It's as if when you try and follow it with your eye it quickly disappears into the mist. As a result you feel a little nervous, not quite sure what qualifies as a fitting response, and not well guided. Your enthusiasm for question one is, at best, low. Question two gives much better direction. It exposes two parallel pathways. The first is a track that invites you to consider which attitudes and behaviors would make you proud. The second track invites you to consider the attitudes and behaviors that would make you excited to work there. The qualifying criteria (proud and/or excited) are clear and both connect with your emotions as something you can feel bothered about. Enthusiasm to question two is higher than our first example.

That said, it might be the case that you don't necessarily want a culture that makes you excited or one in which feeling proud of the organization is a priority. This is fine. But the internal question for yourself as chair and effectively acting as leader in this situation is: What do you want people to have in their heads as they apply energy and thinking to the challenge? Because if you don't place something sticky in the mind of the group, something else will influence the process. It might be a film that someone watched the previous evening; a painting hanging on the wall of the meeting room; the headline of today's newspaper; the final stinging words to an argument that one of the participants had with their husband the previous evening. And as the guardian of the organization; as a well-paid senior executive, it isn't good enough to have important decisions about organizational design driven by nothing more than randomness.

Let us consider some alternative phrasing and construction of some well-worn questions. As you read these, try to judge which give you more energy, which give you clearer and stronger lines along which to travel, and which access and release the body of ideas already in your head to the greatest degree.

Instead of	How can we be more customer-focused?
Try	If we gave our customers everything they wanted, what would we be doing differently?
Instead of	How can we cut costs?
Try	Where in the business can we improve performance solely by cutting costs?
Instead of	How can we make the organization more innovative?
Try	If we could grant everyone in the organization twice as much courage, what would we see that was different?
Instead of	How can we try harder to improve leadership in the organization?
Try	What could we do less of to improve leadership in the organization?
Instead of	Why won't our managers act more corporately?
Try	What are the best reasons we can think of that explain why managers don't act corporately?

Set your thoughts on fire

As the previous section began to suggest, much of the journey toward better thinking is about discovering more helpful aspects of the Sticky Thinking habit so that we can combat the randomness that it brings, and replace it with something altogether more valuable. We can take it as given that the stickiness of words and phrases, whether pack-  aged as questions or even as argumentation will always provide an agenda for thinking and discussion. In a sense, the war is more often than not fought over the stickiness of ideas rather than the merits of those ideas alone. Making thoughts attractive for the right reasons becomes a key step in thinking conversations.

Setting your thoughts on fire has two meanings. The first meaning is that in order to inject energy into a thinking process, to steal the attention of those involved in thinking and most importantly to successfully set up alternative thinking channels, the words, phrases, and expressions that we use need to be incandescent. They need to dance in front of us like flames so that we have no option but to be drawn to them. In this section we will explore how this can be done.

The second meaning of 'setting our thoughts on fire' is that when we are doing this we need to liberate our thoughts and ideas from ourselves. Once they leave our mouths, in fact as soon as they are born, we need to no longer regard our thoughts as belonging to us. If this doesn't happen we spend the entire time backing our own ideas against other potentially better ones provided by other people. In setting our thoughts on fire therefore we are willing to sacrifice them to a greater good, that of higher quality, more energized and better problem solving.

Let us consider some powerful words used in literature, film, and music and judge how well these meet the first criteria of presenting ideas as incandescent propositions:

'*God is dead*'. Friedrich Nietzsche (1844–1900), *The Gay Science*, 1882. Nietzsche proposes here that God is a social construct no longer needed.

'*Anatomy is destiny*'. Sigmund Freud (1856–1939), *Collected Writings*, 1924. Freud proposes here that it is physiological condition and genetic inheritance that shapes our lives.

'*Life's but a walking shadow; a poor player, that struts and frets his hour upon the stage, and then is heard no more: it is a tale told by an idiot, full of sound and fury, signifying nothing.*' – William Shakespeare (1564–1616), *Macbeth* (Act V, Scene V, p. 154). Shakespeare proposes here that we conduct our lives as if we were playing roles and with no greater meaning beyond this.

'*All over people changing their votes, along with their overcoats, if Adolf Hitler flew in today, they'd send a limousine anyway.*' White Man in Hammersmith Palais, The Clash, Columbia (1977). The Clash highlights here the fickle nature of politics.

While different forms of phrasing and expression work differently for different people there is no denying that these examples command attention. If we take, as an example, the explanatory comments that I have provided following each quotation, which in essence capture the meaning of each proposition, we can see clearly that alternative expressions of the same idea can attract entirely different levels of attention and energy. In this case, the more factual accounts of the propositions leave us fairly cold and as presented are less likely to trigger the opening-up of new, better avenues of thinking. Let us take a look at these separately:

1. Nietzsche proposes that God is a social construct that it is no longer needed
2. Freud proposes that it is physiological condition and genetic inheritance that shapes our lives
3. Shakespeare proposes that we conduct our lives as if we were playing roles and with no greater meaning beyond this
4. The Clash highlights the fickle nature of politics

Isn't it remarkable how easily profound thoughts can be turned into a clatter of garbage can lids just with the application of some lifeless words and banal phrasing? What therefore is going on in the construction of more incandescent propositions that make them so irresistible? What can we learn from these and other examples of powerful phrasing? Presented in Table 2.3 are some key ingredients of more fiery propositions that can help us in setting-up better thinking channels.

The first wheel in Table 2.3 provides a guide to the kind of qualities that, if conveyed in thinking conversations, will attract the attention of, and achieve a connection to, those participating. These may not always come naturally to us. Over time though as we practice showing these qualities and find a way of doing so that can be accommodated within our own particular personal style, the results will be startling. Remember too, as the dual meaning of 'setting our thoughts on fire' conveys, this is not simply about finding ways of winning arguments or dominating discussions. It is about drawing the conversation toward more valuable areas of thinking. It's a bit like having a dynamite striker in a soccer match who is lethal providing you can get the ball to them. All of this, in fact everything up until this point in the book, has been about positioning a thinking conversation so that the ball can be set up for a truly breathtaking goal. Showing conviction, passion, courage or any combination of these qualities in the words we use fixes attention on the emerging proposition that can then, and only then, be successfully directed along more profitable thinking channels.

Table 2.3 Ingredients of fiery thinking propositions

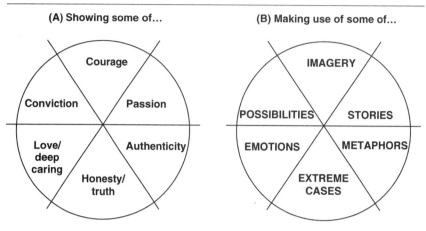

All of our experiences will tell us that some people can be extremely effective if they deploy even one of these features. There are many good leaders that can communicate with such authenticity that they automatically command attention. I can think of one figure in particular, called Robert Swan, OBE, who was the first person in the world to walk to the North and South Pole. His personal honesty in relation to the challenges he faced on returning to 'real-life', his commitment to honoring Sir Robert Scott, who had trod a similar path, and his humility in learning from each and every one of his experiences, causes audiences to cherish every word he says as if it were gold. I know people who have heard Robert Swan talk some fifteen years earlier and can still recall the honesty with which he spoke and the imagery that he conjured up. Part of Robert Swan's success lies too in the thinking channels he offers which are a far call from the basic thinking repertoire in Chapter 1 of this book.

Our second wheel is about achieving the same end but this time the focus is less on what qualities should be conveyed in the words used and more about what resources might be used to greatest effect. For example, in The Clash lyrics shown just before, the use of the image of Adolf Hitler treated to a first class service and being greeted at the airport by a limousine helps to drive a simple point home. Similarly Shakespeare's metaphor of life as being like a stage perform-ance invites us to consider the absurdity of the lives we lead and to do so in a way that may even fix in our minds forever. Both of these propositions are afforded our time and attention because of how they are signaled as much as what they are signaling.

I remember on a number of occasions having invited Sir Tom McKillop, the former Chief Executive Officer of AstraZeneca, to present in various leadership development forums. He is a man that led AstraZeneca to incredible success so that the company delivers pharmaceutical solutions in over 100 countries, achieving sales in excess of $22 billion each year. Tom McKillop is truly impressive in the way he utilizes imagery and emotional language to fix attention on his ideas. One particular notion he refers to is that of 'pushing his company to the creative edge of chaos'. It is a powerful mixture of words that articulates the need for his organization to creatively lead on research to deliver solutions in a volatile and rapidly changing world. The phrasing that he uses engages with us emotionally, it holds a vibrancy and power, and it shows the courage that he and his organization possess.

David Varney, the former Chair of the mobile phone company O_2 and Executive Chair of the 100,000-strong government body, Her Majesty's Customs and Revenue, speaks too with powerful images. In describing the need to be rigorous in the pursuit of creativity and new ways of thinking, David Varney describes the shift in approach to the high jump in athletics which lead from a forward roll to what we now know as the backwards Fosbury Flop. David uses this metaphor to highlight that better levels of performance are not always achieved by doing the same things more effectively; sometimes it's about challenging all of the assumptions we make. This is an image that has never left me and has in effect set up a virtual thinking channel whenever I give me mind over to the subject of creativity.

Let us put all of this back in context for the moment. The point that I wish to make here is that in order to break away from our limited repertoire of thinking habits, we need to put something in its place. In addition to all of the suggestions provided throughout this chapter, such as monitoring thinking habits and creating a helpful environment, we need to lure the discussion into more productive patterns and thinking channels. Doing this means thinking ahead toward where the discussion should be directed; it means purposefully selecting the words that we use; it means framing our questions with great care, and it means using language, ideas, words, and propositions that will ignite the interest of all those involved. If I am a real estate agent trying to sell you a house, I have to get you in there first before there is any chance you will buy it. All of these strategies are about getting people through the front door.

To conclude, the specific benefits of setting our thoughts on fire (using both meanings) are that:

- It releases *energy* into a thinking conversation
- It engages the *emotions* in the thinking process
- It helps to fix **attention** on new channels of thinking
- It helps to fix in our *memory* specific thinking channels (which can help us remember and re-trace our steps)
- It prevents people from becoming too *possessive* of their ideas

Next time you are speaking with colleagues or your staff try to give life to your ideas. Show the conviction you hold; communicate the passion you have, and do so with tantalizing images or metaphors. Like a magnet drawing ironing filings to it, see how you fix attention on your words and see how ready people are to be led down truly valuable thinking channels.

Keep on the move

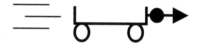

What do all of the following share in common?

Boxers, soccer players, sharks, fugitives from the law, journalists, philosophers, successful businessmen, and adulterers?

The answer is of course that they all need to constantly keep on the move in order to be successful. But actually, that isn't the only correct answer; there are many other possibilities. They are all living things. They all appear in the same sentence. There is more than one of each category. They all need water to exist. They are all mortal. They all contain the letter 's'.

Is that all?

No. They are all comprised of physical matter. They can all be photographed (a bit dangerous for the adulterers though!). They can all be male or female. They exist. They can all be written about ... the list is endless, but is there a point to all of this?

Yes.

While all of these answers are 'correct', there is one answer remaining that I hope has eluded you. This is that during his life, Albert Camus, the French philosopher, has, at one time or another, belonged to each of those categories. He played sports when he was younger, in particular boxing and soccer – where he played in goal. In 1941 he was a journalist and editor for the illegal French underground news-paper *Combat*. He was one of the leading philosophers in the Existentialist movement. He had a number of affairs during his marriage to Francine Faure, including a relationship with Maria Casarès, an actress in some of his plays. And his wife is alleged to have called him 'a shark' for his various extramarital activities.

In setting up this sequence of questions I have tried to illustrate two important points. The first, which is a subsidiary point, is that the language used in the earlier part of this section, that is, the heading 'keeping on the move' followed by words like 'sharks', 'boxers', and 'fugitives from the law', lead you into a particular thinking channel which, in this scenario, most probably pushed you into coming up with the 'wrong' answer. Once you had that answer, you presumably felt your job was done and no further thinking was required. As it happened, the 'correct' answer, and the common theme between all of the factors listed, was Albert Camus, but you had no motivation to find it because you thought you had already got there.

The second and more important point of this illustration is that the serious and real challenges we face in business rarely have singular solutions. Unlike crosswords or quiz games that are designed with a 'correct' and singular answer in mind, or the conundrum that I provided at the start of this section, the problems that we face in business and at home are usually more complex and more capable of being answered in a multitude of ways. Furthermore, adopting a mindset that a singular 'correct' solution must be found is a recipe for paralysis. We are likely to be far more successful if we keep on the move and keep generating possibilities, no matter how imperfect, than if we seek to close in on the 'right solution' from the outset. The 'right solution' approach can only serve to gag people or build up such a level of expectation that only the bravest would dare to crack the problem in one move. As the conundrum shows the 'right solution' approach can also lead away from a whole host of better answers, particularly if the question is framed to provide a false or unhelpful lead.

The implications of this shift in mindset though are perhaps more significant than they initially seem. It means that when we lead thinking conversations and we are hoping to move toward solutions, there is a cast-iron guarantee that most of what we offer will not take us directly to where we want to be. Most of our suggestions, like those in responding to the Albert Camus question, will appear off-target, and therefore be judged to have failed or be wrong. And who is going to knowingly contribute an inadequate solution? So as leaders or chairs or senior players we need to permit people to make 'mistakes' in the name of better problem solving. We need to encourage alternate approaches to problems; we need to welcome half answers and seeds of ideas because these are far more valuable to us. And we need to keep our thinking constantly on the move.

This is not just a discipline we should apply to the leadership role we play in how others think. It applies to us too. So that if we are confronted by a challenge or problem, it will serve us better if we can keep circling the problem and taking different lines of attack. The different lines we use may in themselves be different thinking channels, for example, those outlined in chapter one (Deficit Thinking, Equity Thinking etc.) or those provided in Chapter 3. We must do this though in the full knowledge that it may take us a few attempts before we exact the right line of thinking for the problem.

3 Moving Hearts and Minds

In our day-to-day analysis of problems and challenges we unknowingly adopt thinking habits. One form our habits take is the use of 'thinking channels' along which conversation and analysis flow. Thinking channels by their nature guide and at the same time constrain how a given problem will be treated. They deliver the route to different types of solutions and are one of the main processes we bring to problem solving. However, there are three important problems identified in this book:

a. Thinking channel selection is usually unconscious and unmanaged
b. We typically use a narrow range of channels
c. Our existing narrow repertoire of thinking channels is not enough to tackle the problems and challenges we routinely face

Further to this, I have outlined that there are well-established norms and conventions that shape our social thinking. Discussion, analysis, and most forms of social thinking take place as conversations. Conversations follow a 'turn-taking' fashion and have a momentum and character all of their own. This is important because:

a. Attempts to improve the quality and alter the direction of social thinking must work with, rather than against, the norms of conversation
b. Artificially introduced thinking techniques, which include most creative thinking tools on the market, break the flow of conversation and feel awkward and forced
c. The remedy to this requires a widening of the range of thinking channels we use and a 'natural' introduction of these new channels

This chapter is designed to resolve this conundrum, that of changing our habits of thinking but in a way that plays seamlessly into our existing norms of conversation. Do not expect to be given catchy acronyms or mnemonics, or even a long string of pseudo-scientific concepts. Expect instead some simple and strong strategies for bringing about significantly better problem solving and, importantly, methods that work in practice.

The approach that I recommend requires you to observe three fundamental principles, that you should:

1. focus on the process of thinking (as well as the content)
2. focus on the words you use (when triggering new thinking channels)
3. focus religiously on the purpose of the discussion in which you are engaged

If you can follow these three principles in each thinking conversation you will already be halfway there.

A much broader repertoire

In Chapter 1 we looked at six dominant thinking channels that account for the vast majority of the channels that we use. They possess great power and produce strong thinking. Table 3.1 reminds us of this vital, but narrow, repertoire of thinking channels.

For each of the dominant thinking channels listed above, I propose that there are 'shadow side' functions that remain dormant unless purposefully revived and brought into use. The shadow side is broadly the opposite of each dominant channel. For example, the shadow function of Deficit Thinking is what we can call Strength-Based Thinking, which can bring with it a rich body of untapped data and analytical strength that flows easily and naturally from key trigger

Table 3.1 Dominant thinking channels

- Deficit Thinking
- Rational Thinking
- Common Sense Thinking
- Equity Thinking
- Binary Thinking
- Sticky Thinking

questions such as 'what is working well here?' Table 3.2 lists this underbelly of rarely seen shadow functions.

Table 3.2 Dominant and shadow thinking channels

Dominant function	Shadow function
Deficit Thinking	Strength-Based Thinking
Rational Thinking	Feeling Thinking
Common Sense Thinking	Insight Thinking
Equity Thinking	360 Degree Thinking
Binary Thinking	Re-Integrated Thinking
Sticky Thinking	Exit Thinking

Before explaining how and when these should be used I will outline briefly the qualities of each in the following paragraphs.

Strength-Based Thinking (shadow side of Deficit Thinking)

Strength-Based Thinking is the opposite of Deficit Thinking. It is a vastly under-used thinking channel and accounts for a small minority of thinking in practice. It denotes a search for strength, for what works well in any given situation, and it provides us with some of the best data available on how problems can be solved and changes can be made. If we are looking for solutions it flags up what we need to hang on to. If we are an organization undergoing change it points to the baby that we don't want to throw out with the bathwater. If we are an organization that is successful it is a thinking channel that leads us to why. In seeing the value in what we do and how we do it, we can think about how it can be multiplied, how it can be better leveraged. Strength-Based Thinking injects energy into thinking conversations and builds the confidence of those involved. Its use promotes achievement and pride. It is appreciative in the definitive sense that our assets gain, rather than lose, value. With all of the contributions that Strength-Based Thinking make it is a wonder that as an approach to thinking it is used so sparingly. For all the knock-on and cultural benefits that it possesses it is disappointing too that so few people in leadership positions deploy it as a thinking habit.

A possible explanation for its under-use is that Strength-Based Thinking might be thought of by some as promoting an unrealistic view of the world; the user wearing rose-tinted spectacles or even being positive in a sickly sweet kind of way. These are descriptions that hint at an underlying discomfort with looking for success, almost as if to find fault or pick holes in something shows far greater intellectual rigor. For the British, 'being positive' in anything other than wartime conditions somehow translates into being foolhardy. To be optimistic is seen as hubris. To display a positive attitude is to be false – what else could it be, because sooner or later things will go wrong and isn't it better to be realistic from the start? The British, at times, can be like the Eeyore of the world. However, this is not the place for a deconstruction of the British culture, as fascinating as it would be.

The Strength-Based Thinking approach isn't simply about being positive although a positive attitude is an incredibly powerful and worthwhile position to take in many situations. It is about achieving two objectives. The first is identifying what is working well in any situation or system, that is, scanning for successes, achievements, and progress made. This is not necessarily as straightforward as it seems as the unspoken condition is 'given the context and the challenges that are present, what is working well?' It requires therefore an appreciation of the degree of difficulty faced.

I remember undertaking some evaluative work some years ago looking at government programs to tackle deprivation in some of the worst-affected areas in England. The work had involved detailed examination of similar social and economic regeneration programs around the world ranging from Harlem and the Bronx in New York to the slums of Andhra Pradesh in India. Judging progress proved to be incredibly difficult not least because the circumstances that each area faced were so wildly different. If we take just one of the multiple features of deprivation, that of housing, you can imagine the difficulty in establishing success in housing improvements. Housing prices in England are markedly lower in the North than they are in the South East and as a result the degree of difficulty in improving living conditions is so much greater in London, for example. Harlem has a similar picture to London but a different set of challenges from the North of England and an even greater distance opens up when the comparison is made to the slum dwellings in parts of India. Using our Strength-Based analysis therefore we have to unpick progress and success from a complex picture. In answer to the earlier challenge that Strength-Based Thinking is somehow inferior to more 'intellectually tough' deficit analysis, I would invite those critics to focus their minds on this particular quandary. In short, the job of identifying progress and strength isn't always easy.

The second objective is about understanding why success occurs. Why is General Motors such a successful multi-national company?

Why are some hospitals exemplary in their treatment of patients? What are good fathers doing that makes them successful at parenting? In light of the incredible volume of traffic on our roads, what are we doing right that prevents more accidents from occurring? In light of the remarkable pace of change in technology, what enables us to keep up? In light of the differences between us in terms of wealth, religion, beliefs, and politics, what are we doing right that keeps nations talking to one another, people trading and living conditions improving? This is not to say that there are no flaws or failures in every one of these examples given. It is to say though that if we can understand the root causes of success, we are that much more able to multiply it.

Strength-Based Thinking	What has been working well?
Helpful Questions and Phrases	Despite all of the difficulties we have faced, we have been able to make progress, what has made this possible?
	What has been working well?
	Despite all of the difficulties we have faced, we have been able to make progress, what has made this possible?
	What particular contributions have added to the success of this project?
	What particular features of the environment have helped us?
	What are we most proud of?

Feeling Thinking (shadow side of Rational Thinking)

In the discussion of the Rational Thinking habit outlined in the first chapter to this book, I articulated my anxiety about the way that feelings and emotions, particularly in the work environment, are seemingly removed from the decision-making equation. Our biggest decisions, certainly on a personal level, are shaped by our feelings. The purchase of a home, the choice of holiday, and the decision about whom we marry are all illustrations of this point. In business too our customers and clients are people, who are influenced by emotions and how they feel. Brand managers understand this better than most. Richard Branson's Virgin brand is about fun, modernity, and irreverence. 3M's brand is about technological innovation, solving problems, and creative thinking.

All of these brand ingredients connect to us, as consumers, at an emotional level, and it is in large part our emotional response that guides our purchasing decisions. Furthermore, our companies and our public institutions are staffed by people who do not leave their emotions at home when they shut the front door and travel to work in the morning. To conduct thinking conversations as if emotions don't and shouldn't have a voice is nothing less than perverse.

An illustration of this argument is some work I lead some years ago in examining the UK government's decision to sell two-thirds of its gold reserves, and to re-invest the proceeds in a portfolio of currencies (US dollars, yen, and euros). At one level it was an investigation of the most effective method to sell large quantities of gold into the market so as to maximize revenue. From a different perspective, it was about the relationship that people had with the tangible security offered by gold bars and the symbolic significance of the decision to sell gold reserves. It was such a strongly held view that *The Times* was inundated with letters from appalled citizens who had made a significantly different risk assessment of the decision from the government. The answer to the 'so what?' question, is that considerable support, at least in the early stages, was lost for the government's decision at a fragile point in the process. Criticism from gold-producing countries such as South Africa and South America came thick and fast as they feared this would trigger a major slump in the price of gold. This nervousness ricocheted across the international marketplace and prices went haywire for some months. The combined effect of these emotional as well as rational responses posed a major challenge to the sales program and brought with it variations in revenue in the order of tens of millions of dollars as a result.

We need to re-write emotions back into the script of our thinking conversations. The way we can do this is to use an appropriate thinking channel that will drive thinking along the right track. The difficulties we will encounter in successfully using a Feeling Thinking channel are not related to skill or intellectual complexity, but to the general awkwardness people sometimes experience when feelings surface. I would like to say that is a problem experienced equally by men, as it is by women. However, it's not. The legacy of generations of emotionally cool and invulnerable male figures has made an impact, and our application of this approach needs to bear this in mind.

The key to facilitating Feeling Thinking is to encourage and provide permission to contribute emotional data to a discussion. If we frame emotions and feelings in terms of data or intelligence, we automatically raise their credibility. This may not be necessary for all people, but certainly for many. If too we are willing to objectively map the relationship between emotional data and the operation of a system, for example the impact of morale on productivity, we can hold at bay the deficit desire to judge the emotions presented. All of this may sound a little over-engineered; however, when you are driving in the opposite direction of an organizational norm you need all the help you can get.

Feeling Thinking *Helpful Questions and Phrases*	What does our gut instinct tell us about this situation?
	If we only focus on how we feel about this problem, what will we find?
	What is the likely impact of how people feel about this on the outcome?
	I would like to hear all the data we have on the emotional impact of this situation.

Re-Integrated Thinking (shadow side of Binary Thinking)

The weakness of Binary Thinking, as explored earlier, is that when we come to typify situations as being either/or scenarios, we imply that a both/and characterization is not possible. For example, if we argue that we can either live in the country or live in the city, we exclude the possibility that we can both live in the country and live in the city at the same time. While on one level this makes absolute sense it doesn't necessarily help us in the task of thinking and finding solutions, or in this example, in finding somewhere to live. As we all know there are areas within most cities that have many of the defining features of the country. In the same way, some rural areas have the standards of transportation, shopping, and even nightlife that we associate with the city.

I have no doubt that some people will find this argument unconvincing. But I would like to draw a clear distinction between how we chose to conceptualize reality and the mutually exclusive categories within that reality, and the resources and techniques we draw upon to navigate our way through the world. It is really a question of methodology rather than philosophy. The explicit question being, 'Can it be of use to us if we think about ways to integrate seemingly inconsistent possibilities?' The answer has to be a resounding 'yes'. In fact, not only is this useful, it is an approach that liberates incredible thinking power. Somehow in the clash between two opposites we find so much creativity.

The best way to establish a Re-Integrated Thinking channel is to start with a 'how' question which carries the implication that the question can be answered; it's just a matter of method. We must also bear in mind that the answers we find will act as stepping-stones and that they may not in themselves deliver the definitive answer. All that we discussed earlier about holding off from criticizing half solutions or 'wrong answers' comes into play here.

If we take another example, this time in a business setting, we might ask 'how can this organization take speedy corporate decisions AND consult widely, extensively, and thoroughly on those decisions?' The two ends of this conundrum offer seemingly contradictory and intractable positions. But, do we see ways in which the question might be answered? Below are some stepping-stone possibilities:

Answer	Important decisions could have a pre-announced and well-publicized 'consultation day' when opinion-formers are invited to hold discussions and offer views both physically, in meeting forums, and virtually, through the use of intranets and other electronic means. Feedback on those views and the action taken could be equally rapid
Answer	Organizations could attribute a cost to the elapsed time for decisions and establish a project budget accordingly. Project managers would then be made accountable for cost overruns.
Answer	Staff in organizations could be asked to vote on multiple-choice options in relation to key decisions. Full and comprehensive briefing could be provided up front so that members of staff were informed voters.
Answer	Some corporate decisions in the organizations could be taken quickly by a small number of key stakeholders, and when they are implemented they could be given a temporary status. The organization could effectively try these out in practice, and adjustments and refinements could be routinely made. A benefit of this would be that adjustments to decisions would be based on practical experience and not on theoretical supposition.

A final component of the Re-Integrated Thinking channel is a line of questioning that tackles the issue of contradiction in a different way.

It shares a great deal with a principle used in the martial arts, that of using the strength of your opponent to win. In the martial arts if, for example, your opponent has a heavy build and as a result uses his/her weight to bring you to the ground, then your strategy might be to introduce a manoeuvre where your opponent is forced to lean into you, at which point you quickly move away to allow them to crash to the floor. If your opponent has great speed and agility, you defend for longer than usual so as to tire them out and strike when they are weaker. In both instances you turn the strength of the opposition into your own strength.

Applying this principle to the challenge of thinking and, let's say, taking the same binary positions of speedy decision-making and thorough consultation, we can attempt to make progress in the following way:

Step One: Consult widely on proposals for new methods to speed up decision-making

Step Two: As trust and 'buy-in' increases from widespread consultation, quickly trial these methods

Step Three: Communicate subsequent corporate decisions to the organization more quickly. Highlight the benefits and the consultative process that made it possible

Step Four: Consult again on possible ways to make corporate decision-making quicker etc.

The process is like an upward spiral using the strength of each opposing position to climb upwards. The approach can be applied to a personal level too. For example, if I am shy and want to become more extrovert, the starting question is how can I use my shyness in order to become more extrovert? It sounds unsolvable but perhaps there are qualities of shyness that will help. I will leave this conundrum for you to crack.

Re-Integrated Thinking *Helpful Questions and Phrases*	What are the conditions under which we could have both of these possibilities? What strengths do each opposing positions possess that might be used to solve this problem? What are the strengths of this apparent weakness? What qualities do these opposing positions share?

Insight Thinking (shadow side of Common-Sense Thinking)

How often in a thinking conversation have you heard anyone ask from a group for their practical experience or proven expertise in solving the problem in hand? The Common-Sense channel, which of course contains a large dollop of Equity Thinking, implicitly follows the principle that we all have something to offer; that our collective common sense and knowledge of the world should be enough to overcome the challenge. It's sometimes a bit like shoving a rifle in the arms of young Johnny and saying 'why don't you have a crack it, what's the worst that could happen?' While there may be merits in this strategy, the shadow channel of Insight Thinking may actually hold much better remedies to the problems we face. As with all dominant thinking channels unless we invoke the Insight channel the chances are that we will rely on a common-sense approach with the associated shortcomings explored in Chapter 1.

In the British Civil Service, a body of almost three quarters of a million people, there has been a predominance of a 'generalist' approach to policy-making and implementation. For decades in fact Civil Servants have been valued for their ability to turn their hand to anything from financial management to marketing. Postings within the Civil Service have been predicated on this belief, as have promotions and pay. It has helped to produce some very capable and well-rounded individuals. The Insight Thinking principle though, as with many organizations, has been used as often as a country road in the highlands of Scotland. In the British Civil Service this is changing and the pendulum is starting to swing in a different direction.

Insight Thinking is a call for experience, know-how, and expertise. Unusually it may serve to quieten many people involved in a discussion if they have nothing more than common sense to bring to the table. It is partly this fear of silence that serves to permit the common sense approach. What are required are discipline and an honest exploration of what people really know.

A comparison I would draw is to a passion of mine for SCUBA diving. I have dived now for over 15 years and although I wouldn't describe myself as an expert I have reached a level of experience that gives me enough confidence to know how to dive well. Ironically, 10 years ago I would have claimed the same level of proficiency and understanding but I would have been wrong. What has happened in the decade in between is what we would be interested in if we were to use the Insight channel. For example, I now know that the greatest risks underwater are not from sharks, poisonous fish, or sea snakes, but from currents and poor visibility. I know also that it pays to quickly form a good relationship with the skipper and the dive leader, as these are the people you want to remember you to ensure you are safely returned home. And I know too that attitude is everything. If you are calm, methodical, and peaceful, your air will last longer, you won't panic, and everything will come naturally. If you are nervous and jumpy you will think you are in trouble long before you actually are.

If we are looking for the equivalent in business how are we to draw out real insights if we don't ask for them? How can we differentiate ostensibly sensible, plausible ideas from those born out of hard graft and experience? As employees in knowledge industries flit from company to company how can we make sure we capture and harness expertise? The answer is to purposefully set up Insight Thinking channels in our conversations and, as much as our culture might offer resistance, we should signal that if people don't know the answer they should say so and leave room for those that do.

Insight Thinking *Helpful Questions and Phrases*	How has this problem been solved before? What are the proven remedies? What expertise can we apply to this challenge? What, from experience, do we know really matters here?

360 Degree Thinking (shadow side of Equity Thinking)

As argued in Chapter 1, equity, or fairness, is all a matter of perspective. At times we might find this hard to accept, particularly when we think of fairness in the context of social progress or rights. But fairness is literally about a point of view and where you believe the balance should lie. The problem with the Equity Thinking channel is it is applied as if this weren't the case. It is invoked as if fairness was a natural and unchallengeable position to take – who would be brave enough to say that 'fairness' wasn't important? We do not need to walk over the ground already explored in Chapter 1 other than to say that the shadow function of Equity Thinking is about adopting multiple, rather than single, perspectives on any given problem. Seeing a situation simultaneously from many perspectives and seeking to understand how the picture changes as a result both challenges the equity principle and provides a basis for much stronger decision-making.

Let me illustrate this using the sport of soccer, in particular, the difficult job of refereeing a soccer game. Imagine the scenario where a referee sees a foul on the pitch in the final of an international game. Assume that the player who commits the foul is some 50 yards from the referee and the player is the team's top striker and greatest hope for victory. The referee makes a judgment call and he sends the player off. The cry from the disgruntled team and its supporters is swift. 'It's an outrage!' 'It's totally unfair', 'you can't send off the top player – where's the fairness in that?' Picture what would happen if the team with the sent-off player were to lose, by, say, one goal to nil. 'What a travesty!' 'What a disgrace!' The equity channel, as adopted here, would lead us down the same frustrating dead end time after time. But a 360 Degree Thinking channel gives us so much more to work with (assuming of course we want to do more than let off steam).

Let us replay the scene, this time focusing on the decision from different perspectives:

Focus	Point of view
The injured soccer player	'This is perhaps the most important match I will play in my life. I have trained for this moment for years and I want to win for my country. It is absolutely right that the referee should make the decision he has. Without someone enforcing the rules a match as important as this would be unplayable'
The referee	'While it is never easy to see everything that happens on the pitch, I am confident that I made the right decision. I shouldn't be swayed by the fact that this is the final match or that the player concerned is a top striker. My role is to apply the rules of soccer and everyone on the pitch understands this and knows the risks of breaking them'
The Soccer Association	'We want to represent and protect the sport of soccer for all concerned. We have spent years building the reputation of the game and tackling hooliganism and violence whether on or off the pitch'

| The TV station | 'Our ratings are critical to our success. Dramatic events like this are great' |
| The disqualified player | 'Soccer is a very physical game. Sometimes in the heat of the moment you might play someone's legs instead of the ball, but its not really deliberate. The referee should know this and flex the rules a little. Besides how can he be so sure, he was 50 yards away' |

Adopting the 360 degree channel, as we have done here, changes the picture forever and in doing so enables us to take up a much more 'grown-up' position.

The equivalent process as applied to business is much more than looking at the interests of stakeholders (although this in itself is valuable). In the unforgettable words of Harper Lee in the book *To Kill a Mockingbird* it is about 'walking in someone else's skin' to understand their perspective. This is what the 360 degree channel is intended to achieve.

An application in the workplace might be to the deceptively simple job of giving presentations to audiences large and small. Numerous surveys have shown that next to getting married, public speaking is one of the activities we fear the most. So how might the 360 degree channel help us with this? Invoking the 360 degree channel might invite us to think about the experience from the perspective of the speaker in question, the audience, the technicians, and other speakers (assuming it is a conference or large event).

Individuals vary in their attitude to public speaking but most feel some degree of nervousness, performance anxiety, and in extreme cases, feelings of nausea, breathlessness, and even temporary memory loss. If you recognize any of these stay tuned. Let us assume that **the speaker in question** experiences many of these symptoms. They will no doubt too worry that some members of the audience will make their time on the stage difficult; perhaps because they might think they know more than the speaker, because they are disinterested, or even because they plainly disagree. Much of this 'white noise' serves to unsettle the speaker in question and often turns coherent, well-presented prose into a tangle of wires and fumbled words. But before we decide to pull out of public speaking forever at the prospect of this nightmarish ordeal, let us stop to consider how others might feel.

The audience for most conferences or seminars have different motivations for attending. Some participants are there because they are very keen to learn and borrow from the speakers; others because they want to check out the competition; some are there because it is a nice day out and beats staying in the office, and others are there principally to network and may only have a passing interest in the formal speaking sessions. Expectations are rarely set high across the board and many participants are, at one level, just thankful that they don't have to be there standing up on the stage in the spotlight. Participants at the pre-lunch slots most of all want to get to their food and the audience in the post-lunch 'graveyard' slots are too busy digesting it. The final day of residential conferences will no doubt deliver some people 'tired' from the final night farewells. And as the mid-morning session is underway many will be focused on how to get the coffee they missed at breakfast and when to check out. As the speaker gets on stage half of the audience will be swapping cards and e-mail addresses with their new friends and the other half will be admiring the free pens, pads, and tiepins they have collected.

Minutes before the speaker mounts the stage **the technicians** who once dreamed of being roadies for Bon Jovi will be frantically trying to fix feedback from the main speaker, adjusting fonts on the PowerPoint presentation, and shoving their hands inside the jackets of waiting speakers to attach lapel microphones. At the very last minute a bulb will go in the projector or the screen being lowered down will jam.

The other speakers will be mumbling to themselves and working through their speeches, sharing the same kind of performance anxiety as our speaker in question. Amazing how lonely it can be to have so much in common with other people.

And so how does this form of analysis, this thinking channel, alter the picture? In the first instance, it helps to quieten and reduce the 'white noise' of the presenting problem – that of an overwhelming fear of public speaking. Adopting a 360 degree perspective shows that there is so much going on in the scene that for the speaker to be pre-occupied with the fear of performing, is to over focus on only one of the many dramas being played out. Expressed simply, what appears to be an issue of huge significance to the speaker is shared by no one else in the room. It is like driving at high speed around to a friend's house for dinner, breaking the speed limit, and getting a ticket, only to realize that when you get there it started later than you thought. Secondly, the Equity Thinking channel, our default position, helps to fuel the internal struggle and worry we harbor when approaching public speaking. This is because unconsciously we compare our own discomfort and anxiety with the relaxed state of the audience and see a yawning gap. The cards seem stacked heavily in favor of 'them' and that is just 'plain unfair!' In short, the Equity Thinking channel can exacerbate the problem where 360 Degree Thinking gives us the data and confidence to move forward. 360 Degree Thinking gives the picture much better resolution – it's like shifting from black and white to color television.

360 Degree Thinking	How would others see this?
Helpful Questions and Phrases	Who would have a justifiable reason for seeing this differently?
	Let's hear all the possible perspectives on this

Changing channels

Our habits lead us, by default, to the thinking channels explored in Chapter 1. This book has set out to name them and make them more visible to us. In thinking conversations as we see these channels arising we can chose to let them run for as long as they prove useful to us and deliver the benefits inherent to each track. It is important to remember that each of the thinking channels examined in Chapter 1 carries great power, and this book has not sought to demonize our dominant habits. But, as the benefits of each channel are released, we need to be prepared to move the conversation to more fruitful pastures, which, in the main, are the shadow channels we have just discussed. We need also to think about how thinking channels can be used to shift the way in which people engage with the problems and challenges they face. We need to consider how thinking channels can be deployed to create movement, to achieve buy-in, to release energy, and to lead to action. We need to consider how leaders can shift the thinking of others through the channels they trigger. We need to harness thinking channels to move the hearts and minds of others.

What follows are methods to achieve this – three simple strategies for introducing these channels naturally into conversation. These are designed so that you will have no difficulties remembering them and so that you are left with as much scope as possible to then focus on the content of your discussions. Over time you should aim to master all three approaches – the third being the most powerful:

- channel flipping (very easy)
- channel hopping (easy)
- remote control (moderate).

Channel flipping (very easy)

Think of each channel as like a coin. On one side is the dominant thinking channel and on the other side, the shadow thinking channel. The first role we can play in the course of thinking conversations is to intervene to flip the coin and ensure that, in sequence, we see both sides and both thinking channels. **In doing so we immediately double the quality and strength of our thinking and, in an instant, change the way people see a given problem.** For example, if the discussion is about how to improve the marketing of a product we may witness the silent selection of the Deficit Thinking channel. Someone might say, 'the problem is that people always confuse our brand with the competition. We just don't differentiate ourselves well enough' [Deficit Thinking]. Our aim in this scenario would be to allow this channel to fill up with data and analysis until we judge that nothing new is being added. When this point is reached we should flip the channel and introduce the opposite shadow function, in this case Strength-Based Thinking. In terms of how this method works, all that we have to be able to do is to identify the channel in use and trigger the opposite channel – what could be easier? The trigger question might be as simple as 'this has been really useful. Could we explore though what we are doing right? What do we really value about our current marketing strategy?' The change in direction honors both sides of the coin and immediately enhances the thinking process. It also occurs as a natural shift in the discussion and as a result will be accepted. In the next conversation you have try it for yourself and notice how easy it is to do and how much stronger the analysis becomes.

Taking this example a little further, what would follow from this change in direction? We might witness a search for the root causes of success (rather than failure); the segments of the market that do recognize the brand and don't confuse it with the competition; where success has been achieved in previous marketing campaigns. When you then set side by side the two types of data generated by each channel you see how important it is to deliberately flip the channels. You collectively have a much better basis for making decisions. Table 3.3 illustrates some of the key points that might emerge.

The remainder of the discussion might then involve understanding what has been working well with the lower-income customer group. It might be to explore whether further simplifying the offering might help to differentiate the product. The answer to the problem might be to work out why the marketing team were able to hold off the competition's last major campaign.

Table 3.3 Channel flipping — Deficit Thinking and Strength-Based Thinking

Deficit Thinking channel (Taking marketing example)	Strength-Based Thinking channel (Taking marketing example)
• Low brand recognition	• Good brand recognition among lower-income customers
• Insufficient brand differentiation	
	• Last marketing campaign held off recent launch of competitors new product
• Similarity with competitor products	
• Marketing has too low priority in the organization	• New structure within marketing team working well
• Insufficient skills of marketing team	• Previous campaign successfully simplified the offering

The fundamental approach in this and other thinking conversations is to first find a point at which the existing channel is full and then trigger the flipside channel. This is sometimes easier said than done particularly with channels that, by their nature, have great longevity such as the Deficit or Equity Thinking channels, or where the shadow channel can be harder to access such as Feeling Thinking (often because feelings can strike some as inappropriate in business meetings). **One essential piece of advice I would give in doing this is that before you trigger the flip side channel, you should first validate the dominant channel**. I would remind you of the first few words used in the previous example to achieve this movement: '*this has been really useful*. Could we explore though what we are doing right? What do we really value about our current marketing strategy?' It will be a far smoother transition if you show support to what has just occurred.

Once we have successfully triggered a change in channel, we need to keep the discussion firmly slotted in the shadow channel. Our dominant habits have a magnetic quality that tends to wrench the conversation back into the original channel, at which point everyone else will pile in afterwards. We need to exercise discipline and pick our words carefully. Neutral, vague, or generally expressed questions such as 'what else do we think about this?' will not possess enough power and keep people in the shadow channel. The helpful questions and phrases listed in Table 3.4 should help you keep the discussion on track. As someone taking responsibility for high-quality social thinking, words and language are your most powerful tools. Channel flipping is the easiest of our three strategies.

Table 3.4 Trigger questions for shadow thinking channels

Shadow thinking channel	Trigger questions	Dominant thinking channel
Strength-Based Thinking	• What has been working well? • Where have we made progress? • What are we most proud of?	Deficit Thinking
Feeling Thinking	• What does our gut instinct tell us? • How do we feel about this problem? • What is our emotional response to this?	Rational Thinking
Re-Integrated Thinking	• How could we have both of these possibilities? • What strengths do these opposing positions share? • What if we could have both?	Binary Thinking
Insight Thinking	• How has this problem been solved before? • What do we know, from experience, matters here? • What are the proven remedies?	Common Sense Thinking
360 Degree Thinking	• How would others see this? • Who would see this differently? • Could we hear all of the possible perspectives on this?	Equity Thinking

Channel hopping (easy)

I have the pleasure of owning two cats that have lived with me for many years. In each house I have occupied, the cats have made the garden into their territory. They have frolicked there, sat on the fence posts on hot sunny days, and, as the winter has come and gone, have hidden in the long grass and hunted for mice and shrews. The stunning visual record of their habits has always struck me; in the long grass there has always been a single trench where they have repeatedly flattened the grass. Running from one corner of the garden to the other is a visible pathway that no doubt helps them traverse the garden quickly if being chased or hearing the noise of food being shaken into their bowls.

This pathway can be seen as a metaphor for our dominant thinking channels; they are familiar, well worn, efficient, and useful at getting us quickly from A to B. So what could be wrong with this? Every now and then, the cats find themselves broadening their search for mice and in their devilish pursuit of all things small and prey-like they sometimes wander into the territory of neighboring cats. With a frantic scrabbling of claws on a fence and a rustling of bushes one of them will return at high speed into the house with a bigger cat close behind. The major problem though is that they always use the same carefully trodden pathway to get to the cat flap; even it involves a panic-ridden detour and a few precious extra seconds. The pathway that once served to hasten their escape becomes a barrier to their feline success.

Getting into the habit of routinely hopping between different channels is absolutely essential. In our thinking conversations it is better to keep moving than to turn a shallow thinking channel into a crevasse with mile-high walls. Our role in channel hopping is to actively kick the conversation into new channels. We should bear in mind that no channels are bad channels. All possess problem-solving power and all deliver valuable data to help make smarter decisions. **Channel hopping involves waiting until sufficient intelligence has been gathered using the channel in play and then driving the conversation into any other unused channel.** The only condition is that you should aim to hop into one or more of the shadow channels since the dominant thinking channels usually need no encouragement. They are like the grass that grows between paving stones. Cut it down, turn your back for five seconds and new shoots have already emerged. Channel hopping is a positive stance on randomness and locating new data whatever its source.

Let me give an example. Imagine a discussion about the introduction of a competency framework into a business. The framework would provide explicit areas of skill, knowledge, and behavior against which staff would be assessed. Assume a discussion begins with an Equity Thinking channel: 'we have an incredibly wide range of staff within the company all of which do different jobs and operate at different levels. Any competency framework we use would need to be sophisticated enough to take account of this variability and provide a level playing field for judging performance.' Channel hopping would require us to call, at random, on any of the other shadow channels and successfully drive data into them. The shadow channels we have at our disposal are:

- 360 Degree Thinking
- Strength-Based Thinking
- Insight Thinking

- Feeling Thinking
- Re-Integrated Thinking.

Let us take the last two thinking channels to develop the discussion. Table 3.5 illustrates the trigger questions that would be needed to set up each channel and the data that might be produced.

This could be done just as easily using any of the other shadow channels. In this illustration the data that has been created provides a strong basis on which to take the discussion forward. The ideas have been laid out in front of us like dishes at an all-you-can-eat buffet and all we have left to do is select those that meet our needs.

One tip I would give in this phase of sifting ideas is to make full use of the Deficit Thinking channel. In the process of identifying which ideas will work in practice the deficit habit cannot be beaten. Think of the deficit channel as the final test for a group of potential remedies.

Applying the approach of channel hopping is very straightforward and has the important benefit that it guarantees the use of shadow thinking channels that, under normal circumstances, would not see the light of day.

Remote control (moderate)

Isn't the relationship that some men form with their TV remote controls remarkable? These days, with so many electrical items attached to the TV, it is not uncommon to see a bank of remote controls lined up on the arm of a big comfy chair. Like Yul Brynner in the *Magnificent Seven* the average man can draw and zap the TV in under a second. I know of some men who have turned TV-watching into an art form; their knowledge of scores of channels is unimaginable; the precise start and finish times of a vast array of programs unmatched. The numbers of hundreds of pages corresponding to TV Text service catalogue mentally stored away and selected at a moments notice.

This intimate understanding of each TV station is exactly what is needed with the remote control technique. The previous two approaches of channel flipping and channel hopping require a basic appreciation of the qualities of each shadow channel. Remote Control is about exercising mastery over the twists and turns of any conversation. It is about drawing down from a mental library of channels to shape conversations and get the best from them. **It is what**

Table 3.5 Illustration of channel hopping addressing development of competency frameworks

Dominant channel	Shadow channel (A)	Shadow channel (B)
Equity Thinking	**Feeling Thinking**	**Re-Integrated Thinking**
'How can we ensure there is a level playing field?'	'How are staff likely to feel about this proposition?'	'How can we have both a single standard framework and one that allows for different job types?'
• In the design phase, gain representation across the organization	• Staff will need to feel confident in the system	• The framework could contain a common core with variant additional competencies
• Weight the importance of each competency according to each job type	• Some staff will feel threatened by the new arrangements	• Local areas could be free to determine their own additional competencies beyond the core
• Consider using a 360 degree reporting framework	• Most staff will find the uncertainty of the transition difficult (and a distraction from day-to-day work)	• In the performance assessment process different business units could come together to moderate the scores
• Ensure all levels, including the top, are covered by the framework	• Staff will need to feel it is worth the effort otherwise they will resist	• Training could be provided internally so that standardized elements are fully understood

skilled leaders should do to move the hearts and minds of their people.

If we exclude Sticky Thinking for the time being (to be dealt with later), this leaves 10 thinking channels that we have in our armory. Knowing when they should be used is the name of the game (Table 3.6).

Injecting energy into conversations

Conversation is perhaps one of the most widespread and important activities in which we engage. Every day of our lives we build relationships, share information, develop ideas, shape decisions, solve

Table 3.6 Particular qualities possessed by thinking channels

Qualities (1)	Qualities (2)	Most appropriate thinking channels
ENERGY	Generating energy (conversational fuel)	• Strength-Based Thinking • Feeling Thinking • Re-Integrated Thinking
IDEAS	Generating ideas and possible solutions	• Insight Thinking • Strength-Based Thinking • 360 Degree Thinking • Re-Integrated Thinking
	Generating breakthrough Ideas	• Strength-Based Thinking • Re-Integrated Thinking
BUY-IN	Achieving buy-in to new ideas and strategies	• Feeling Thinking • Strength-Based Thinking • 360 Degree Thinking • Common Sense Thinking
IDEA SIFTING	Sifting ideas and possibilities	• Deficit Thinking • Feeling Thinking
IMPLEMENTATION	Easy implementation of new ideas and strategies	• Insight Thinking • Strength-Based Thinking

problems, hatch plans, express feelings, and much more, all through conversation. Conversation is the engine that drives our thinking and like all engines it needs fuel and energy to keep it going. Often in conversations we can find ourselves becoming sapped of energy and as this occurs our engagement with the issues raised disappears. This has a lot of causes ranging from the quality of the discussion to the time of the day. In my experience of having facilitated hundreds of 'brainstorming' events I have found myself focusing more and more on the flow of energy within a room. It is of course invisible to us and we have to take readings from shifts in body posture, voice inflection, noise levels, and the pace of discussion. It always amazes me how much time (and money) can be burnt through sloppy chairing and poor attention to energy management. On the upside (please note, this is an example of channel flipping), I have been staggered by how much can be achieved by people if they are fully engaged in a subject through strong and thoughtful facilitation. If discussions can be made exciting, meaningful and dynamic people will move the earth for you. Where people feel empowered and challenged they will produce gold.

How, then, can we liberate energy and muster engagement? The answer is, through purposeful deployment of thinking channels. The most powerful channel in this respect is Strength-Based Thinking, notably when we can connect it to feelings of pride, accomplishment, or success. It works by demonstrating what can be achieved. When engaged in the problem-solving phase of a discussion what worries us most is the fear that our ideas will come to nothing, that we will fail. Strength-Based Thinking shows us, beyond doubt, that we can be triumphant. It moves us from theory to a reality we desire. There is nothing like confirmatory evidence to lift the spirits and jump-start the batteries.

Feeling Thinking is another energy-creating channel that works by tapping into a different side of our psyche. There is little as interesting to people as themselves. Having put many people through 360 degree diagnostics I can vouch for the hours of study people will devote to every single word written about them. It isn't that we are self-obsessed, although for many it certainly can be a theme; it is more that 360 degree reports invite us to understand ourselves, to discover what we really are and how we feel about that identity. As a consequence I have known people change their jobs, begin diets, join the gym, commit to seeing their family more often, renew their wedding vows, and even emigrate. This is because when we engage our emotions and explore, at a deep level, how we really feel we suddenly become energized, even re-born. The Feeling Thinking channel helps to remove the glass between ourselves and the world around, between what we do and why we do it.

A final method for releasing energy into thinking conversations is through the Re-Integrated channel. For most this is a difficult channel to operate. The challenge of using the Re-Integrated channel lies in skillfully framing 'dilemmas' so that we can resolve the both/and question. The Re-Integrated Thinking channel is designed to help us find the conditions under which we can enjoy both ends of a polarity. It needs therefore to be used appropriately and not simply as a device for injecting energy into a discussion. Assuming though that its use makes sense, the very introduction of two apparently contradictory perspectives accompanied by an invitation to synthesize them creates an irresistible challenge. Like a gauntlet slapped around our cheeks we relish the opportunity to crack the quandary that we face. The trigger question is usually 'how can we have both x and y?' with x and y standing for a variety of conundrums such as full consultation and quick results, change and stability, and standardization and tailoring.

Often after a slow start Re-Integrated Thinking accelerates the discussion and ideas flow thick and fast. We will explore this channel a little more later.

If we are leading change within organizations we have to pay attention to the level of engagement with, and energy generated by, the change agenda. People affected by change quickly become frustrated by central edicts handed down from on-high within organizations, and change leaders therefore need to engender excitement through formal and informal means such as routine conversations. But in order to be successful in doing this all change leaders, agents, and supporters need to know which channels will promote energy and how to introduce and manage these channels 'naturally'.

Generating ideas, new possibilities, and breakthrough thinking

In the same vein as George Orwell's *Animal Farm*, all thinking channels are equal but some are more equal than others. In the context of channels that help create ideas this is particularly true. The four channels highlighted in Table 3.7 have particular strengths in this regard and can be placed on a continuum from those channels that trigger proven remedies and fully worked-up ideas to those that offer powerful ideas that need developing. Table 3.7 shows this continuum.

In establishing channels on the left-hand side, we are seeking ideas that reflect proven experience, expert knowledge, and multiple perspectives. On the right-hand side we are looking to piece together new ideas and solutions from successes elsewhere and from the provocative clash of opposing concepts. Breakthroughs, by definition, tend to arise from new and unproven ideas, particularly where we can crack the seemingly unsolvable dilemmas produced by Binary Thinking.

Let us work through an example of how we can use Re-Integrated Thinking to generate breakthrough ideas. Imagine that an organization is introducing a change program to re-orientate the organization to the

Table 3.7 A continuum of thinking channels from proven ideas to breakthrough, less proven ideas

needs of the customer. Let us assume that the organization hasn't in the past had to work too hard to find customers (perhaps it is in a dominant market position, or perhaps it is a public sector body). The situation has changed though and the organization now needs to change its strategy. One way to conceptualize the problem is to start with the binary view, which is: it's all well and good to meet every need of the customer but what about the needs of employees? If customers want a 24-hour service how does this fit with the needs of staff? If customers want instant responses to any complaints or queries they might have, how can employees do this alongside the 'day job'? If the organization works to the principle that the customer is always right, what happens when the customer is categorically, undeniably, and comprehensively wrong?

A simple way to capture this binary position is to think of one end of the pole being 'the customer comes first' and the other as 'the employee comes first'. So, using this framing of the problem, how can we move towards some innovative ideas? Let us first elaborate on the implications of accepting each pole, as illustrated in Table 3.8.

In adopting the Re-Integrated Thinking channel the question would be 'how can we have both sides of this contradiction?' A discussion would be along the lines of 'under what conditions could both sides of this equation be met?' Let us take each element in turn and generate some initial possibilities:

1. **Provide a 24-hour service <u>AND</u> provide only 9–5 weekday availability**
   - Have two sets of offices dealing with service; one in the home country working 9–5 weekdays and one in another country covering the remaining hours
   - Provide automated services in the evenings and at weekends

Table 3.8 Illustrative binary positions of customer first vs. employee first

Customer comes first	Employee comes first
• 24-hour service provided	• Available during weekdays 9–5
• Instant response to complaints and queries	• Quick response where possible
• Customer always right	• Case-by-case consideration of who is 'right'

2. Provide instant responses to queries <u>AND</u> provide only quick responses where possible

- Pre-prepare/standardize the range of potential remedies to problems so that queries are resolved quickly. Staff would, in essence, choose from a pick list of answers and solutions
- Have a sophisticated filtering system, similar to calling the emergency services, that enables the 'operator' to assess the degree of urgency of each enquiry and, with the agreement of the customer, provide an appropriate response time

3. The customer is always right <u>AND</u> the customer may be right depending on circumstances

- Do not focus on the cause of the issue/complaint and attempt to apportion responsibility (customer vs. company) but instead focus solely on remedies (which removes the question of who is right)
- The company could take responsibility for having exemplary processes so that disagreements themselves have well-established channels. As a result staff employed by the company follow the agreed protocol and do not feel that they need to exercise their own judgment with regard to right and wrong.

Adopting the Re-Integrated Thinking channel moves thinking towards unseen possibilities. Many of these possibilities will be stepping-stones to other more suitable ideas and in this example we can see that some new strategies are already taking shape. A further advantage of using this approach is that in the act of creating possibilities participants in the thinking process find solutions to organizational dilemmas. They become authors of the future and with it can begin to create it. Leaders that want to empower their staff and arm them to move the organization forward can release incredible potential through using this approach.

Achieving buy-in to new ideas and strategies

Securing buy-in to new ideas and strategies is an age-old challenge for organizations seeking to bring about changes in thinking and behavior. Often what people object to most when faced with new ways of conducting business is not the change itself but coercion – the experience of being forced down a particular route without the opportunity, in very simple terms, to have a proper, honest conversation about it. This may sound almost too simple but it is exactly what senior people should pay attention to both at the level of process (social thinking) and content of the change. Engagement with high-quality thinking processes will foster buy-in and support for new strategies. The problem is that so many 'conversations' about change or new ideas aren't conversations at all. Instead they involve the dispensation or delivery of 'the message'; they involve the worst kinds of Sticky and Deficit Thinking where people become stuck in every possible concern and worry about a new strategy; they are conducted without an appreciation of how thinking channels underpin the flow of ideas and feelings.

If you are a leader, an organizational development expert, a change agent, a senior manager, an HR consultant, or anyone seeking to bring about change you should sharpen your skills and master the following thinking channels:

- Feeling Thinking
- Strength-Based Thinking
- 360 Degree Thinking
- Common Sense Thinking

Let us work through each of these of these channels and consider what they are asking us to do in a change process:

Feeling Thinking: we are invited in the early stages of a change program to consider how we feel about the issues presented and the possibilities available. In doing so we commence an exploration of not only an emotional response to the situation but a deeper examination of what we are really here to achieve. This is exactly where discussions need to be kept and what leaders of organizations should be stimulating. In terms of buy-in, if we can operate at this level of discussion we begin to see deeper connections to one another. The marketing guy suddenly connects with the finance guy because they both joined the organization with high aspirations and a hope of making an impact on the world. The sales team share with the operations people the need to really understand the customers and to work as a bigger team. The Feeling Thinking channel engenders buy-in because it fosters connectivity and it treats change with the level of seriousness it deserves.

Strength-Based Thinking: we are invited to imagine success and to discover where excellent results have been achieved elsewhere. In the context of change programs or the pursuit of new strategies and ideas, this channel builds strength and staff that feel strong and able to take on the world. Following the principle of only starting arguments you know you can win, Strength-Based Thinking ensures we win every time.

360 Degree Thinking: we are invited to see change or new ideas as they affect a broad spectrum of people. Because change is always difficult and messy it is almost too easy for those leading the change agenda to become tired of the resistance they always find and simply push harder and faster to make the change happen. The problem with this is that change affects people, and the organizational departments in which they work, very differently. Whereas the HR department might accept the change or even have partly engineered the new agenda, the post room might be incensed by the impact on the staff's location. Where the IT people feel untouched by the change, the marketing people might be pulling their hair out because they now have to recall their promotional literature which has just announced a direction out of line with the new strategy.

This insensitivity to different positions reminds me of the equal opportunity and diversity questionnaires that new employees used to complete perhaps 15 or more years ago. In these very early days, the universe of possible ethnic origins seemed to comprise 'white' or 'non-white.' I can still remember a form asking this very question. The questionnaire, although I am sure invested with good intent, did not take a 360 degree view of the people the company was dealing with. Nowadays of course this is unimaginable and there is rightly a diverse range of options that correspond much more closely to the ethnic make-up of most modern societies.

Common Sense Thinking: we are invited to think about a change agenda in grounded, practical terms. We are invited to consider the fundamental strengths or otherwise of the case for change. If people feel, at this common sense level, that the change agenda makes good sense, the battle is already half won. If sound, common sense arguments can be made in favor of change, and if people can readily see that there are strong foundations to the new agenda this will give the process momentum. Good examples of this are instances where organizations have no choice other than to change – if the workforce are faced with the common sense argument that the market no longer needs what the company is selling; that office rental prices have become prohibitively high; that clear cost-efficiencies can be made by merging departments. Change in this context is much easier to manage but the thinking process has to be driven along the common sense channel in order to get there.

The sequencing of these channels can sometimes be important, and the arrangement above of Feeling Thinking followed by Strength-Based Thinking, 360 Degree Thinking, and finally Common Sense Thinking is a good approach. This works because:

- Feeling Thinking permits people to express deeper, heartfelt issues about the situation. If this channel is held back until a later stage, particularly if the change intended or the ideas proposed trigger a strong reaction, participants will feel deprived of the opportunity to say what they feel. For many people this can be a deal breaker and unless they can articulate their feelings early on, they will either disengage from the discussion, seek to sabotage the discussion (because of their frustration at having their feelings denied), or screen out all of the rational arguments presented.
- Strength-Based Thinking is useful as a follow-up channel because it introduces a sense of hope, possibility, and proof that success is attainable. It is an antidote to the negative feelings sometimes generated in the previous channel. It reminds us that over the years we have successfully adapted and made changes. Strength-Based Thinking in discussion provides a psychological safety net that tells us we can be successful again, which in turn injects much-needed energy into the remainder of the discussion.
- 360 Degree Thinking then moves us into considering the full implications of any change or new ideas. It is a serious thinking channel that invites us to consider what the change or ideas really mean in practice. At this point in the discussion after deeper feelings have been raised and validated, and after a sense of hope and energy has been re-introduced, participants are ready to consider the change in its fullness and to begin to build strategies that address the positions of each point of the compass.
- Finally, the discussion can begin to reach a point of closure where those engaged can articulate what the new ideas or the changes mean in everyday terms. It is like the calm after the storm where a complex web of feelings and ideas is reduced to a set of simple notions. It is where we begin to internalize what has been discussed and to regard the conclusions reached as common sense. After this stage is complete participants in the discussions have a readily understood and clear language that can help to spread the change agenda.

Sifting ideas and possibilities

The skill of checking for flaws that is central to Deficit Thinking is found in abundance within us all. It is useful to us in many situations and is excellent in helping to sift emerging ideas and possibilities. What it helps us to do is gauge the level of risk associated with different options, whether these are solutions to problems or strategies for achieving change. What is important though when sifting ideas with Deficit Thinking is to communicate to those engaged in the process that all changes and all ideas carry risks. It is important to communicate too that our ability to find risks, flaws, and deficiencies is almost infinite. We are simply great at this. Let me demonstrate this by permitting you to 'go to town' in finding risks and flaws with some established and successful solutions, all of which millions, and in some cases billions, of people have made use of. I have provided my assessment of risks relating to one category. Perhaps you could choose another and do the same:

Established idea/solution	Risks/flaws/deficiencies
• Air travel	................................(try yourself)
• The Internet	................................(try yourself)
• Marriage	................................(try yourself)
• Post-Its	................................(try yourself)
• Buying a car	Costly to insure, sale value falls rapidly, you walk/exercise less, you can't drink at parties, petrol prices keep rising, in cities cars are often accidentally damaged, cars have to be serviced annually, cars aren't good for the environment, its often difficult to find parking spaces, traffic wardens are increasingly persistent, you have to pay tax on cars, cars need to be cleaned regularly, the traffic jams in many towns, cities and countries are infuriating, there are increasing numbers of police speed cameras on the roads ...

Given that the Deficit Thinking channel is an excellent sifting approach, but one that needs to be used thoughtfully, a very useful alternative is the Feeling Thinking channel. I am reminded of those familiar words in cowboy films where the hero will walk into a seemingly desolate frontier town with tumbleweeds drifting across the dry sandy road and say, 'it's quiet here; almost too quiet'. This is an excellent example of Feeling Thinking. It is a judgment that comes from the gut. A judgment that is hard to trace but somewhere within the being of the hero, he knows that something is out of place, and usually he is right. When dealing with new ideas or even proposed change initiatives it is enormously useful to ask the questions 'What do we feel about this? What does our gut instinct tell us?'

I imagine the collection of thoughts and feelings related to a particular situation as like an iceberg. Poking out of the top of the water, the tip of the iceberg, is the gut feeling: 'it's too quiet' or 'this doesn't feel right' or 'this feels like it's going to work.' But beneath the tip in the deep, cold water is a web of connected data that we need to dive down to if we are to truly understand the relative strengths of a given proposal. For most people this very powerful trigger question commences a journey, as we often don't fully understand what causes our gut instinct or deeper feelings. The question is often greeted by a raising of eyes up to the sky, a puzzled look descending on the face, or a leaning back in chairs. This is exactly what you want to see and what will give you some fantastic data on whether an idea or proposal will be successful. The role of the leader of the social thinking group, whether it is a chair or a senior figure, is to frame questions in precisely the right way to engender this response. Any clumsiness with words selected will, without doubt, evoke the Deficit Thinking channel with its incumbent strengths but all its weaknesses.

Replacing Sticky Thinking with Exit Thinking

Sticky Thinking is not so much a thinking channel as it is a topic selector. It is one of the least managed but most influential forces in the process of social thinking. By its nature it serves to compete with the three methods I have proposed of channel flipping, channel hopping, and remote control. In every single situation where people come together to think it exercises a kind of random control over the proceedings. I say 'tomato' and you think 'what's for dinner?' You say 'potato' and I am thinking of my trip to Idaho, dubbed 'the potato state'. It may sound odd and it is, but it's just the way that we think.

In order to reign in control over the thinking process we need first of all to be mindful about our use of thinking channels. We need to take the effort to deploy the methods of channel selection discussed so far. These will, at a fundamental level, shape the tone and character of the discussion. But in doing so we need also to mentally fix our destination in mind. Imagine an arrow with a long line of rope attached to the flight. In conversation we should fire the arrow to hit our destination and use the line as our guide rope. Most conversations are more like firing a spray of arrows that lead to everywhere and nowhere. Social thinking should be seen as the process we adopt to help pull ourselves towards our destination and not as an excuse to drink coffee or pass the time of day.

If we are to wrestle control from Sticky Thinking and apply rigor to social thinking we need to pay specific attention to the following:

- **What is realistically achievable in the time available?** Most chairs or leaders of meetings are poor at gauging what it is possible to achieve by the time a meeting has been adjourned. More often than not insufficient time is given to important issues, and on less critical areas, conversation is allowed to wander unchecked for what can seem like days. An old boss of mine used to congratulate himself for the way that he would run meetings as if they were military operations. Agenda timings were sometimes specified to the strangest level of detail, for example '10.32–10.48: Develop strategic approach.' Week after week the second half of meetings would be rushed due to insufficient time and 'Any other Business' would be dealt with as people were running out of the room desperate to get to their next meetings or just to get some fresh oxygen. The upside of this approach was that Sticky Thinking barely got a look-in. The downside of course was that neither did any other kind of thinking. How often have you found yourself in this kind of meeting?
- **What will those engaged in the discussion believe that they are there to achieve?** It is fascinating to me that so many formal and informal thinking discussions take place where those participating do not understand what is expected of them. I am sure that if we could tune in to peoples' thoughts as meeting after meeting trundled by we would very often hear something like 'this is all very interesting but why am I here?' or 'perhaps I should say something somehow relating to the last point'. Talk can sometimes be so cheap that I would rather listen to some elevator music or whale sound. The reason for this deflationary pressure on the currency of

talk is that people usually don't know what their job is and someone needs to tell them. In the meetings or discussions you have
participated in how often are you clear what you, in particular, are
there to do?

- **Who is going to take responsibility for keeping the conversation on target?** For every meeting or purposeful gathering of
  people, demonstrable benefits should arise. If this doesn't happen,
  then at best it has been an opportunity to get to know people better but at worst it has been a waste of time, money, and energy. An
  interesting comparison to make to social thinking is that of the
  rigor applied to most major projects or change management programs which have a distinct stage or chapter that by various names
  is referred to as 'benefits realization'. To my mind it is a wonderful
  notion. It supposes that in order for a project to be truly successful
  effort needs to be focused on realizing the benefits that were
  originally intended at the outset. While one school of thought
  might argue that benefits should flow naturally from the careful
  design and execution of the project, experience tells us that specific
  attention and energy needs to be invested in making sure this happens. The point is that unless someone takes responsibility for this
  in the process of social thinking, the discussion will wander off
  course. How many meetings have you attended where the discussion is steered more by the group than it is by the chair?

The habit of Exit Thinking addresses these three elements. In essence,
it signals a disciplined focus on the exit point for any thinking discussion. It is worth remembering that Sticky Thinking will always occur.
As with the solutions already proposed in this book, there is no point
in attempting to introduce artificial remedies that break conversational norms. This kind of approach simply won't stick. The methods
used to bring about Exit Thinking need to be seamlessly introduced,
particularly where thinking discussions are neither formal activities,
such as meetings, or planned events.

Fortunately, at some time we all have experienced well-run and
successful discussions that demonstrate some or all of these three
components. Such occasions are hugely rewarding and stay with us
for some time. I remember a single meeting I had called with a colleague where she, unprompted, started the meeting by outlining what
she understood as the exit-objective of the discussion (which corre-
sponded with mine), the contribution that she felt she could make,
and her commitment to help make the discussion a successful meeting. It was a great beginning and as the process developed we found

ourselves motoring through the issues and comprehensively delivering against our agreed objective. What was perhaps most surprising about this was that the colleague in question was attending a performance appraisal meeting and had been aware from a previous discussion that she was going to be given a verbal warning. It may have been the serious nature of the discussion that focused her mind but nevertheless the quality of the discussion that took place was unmatched. Once there was crystal clarity on the purpose and the roles to be played and a commitment to make it happen, everything else slotted into place. The 'white noise' present in most discussions was quietened leaving both of us to focus on the job in hand.

Chairing or otherwise leading meetings is a deceptively difficult job – not only because you need to understand the power of thinking channels, and not only because you need to understand the incredible influence of individual words and phrases, and not only because you need to understand the social norms of interaction, but because people are free agents with the right to say anything they choose. When you multiply this right by the number of people participating in any discussion you are only ever a few steps away from chaos. Its not so much a question of herding cats as opening all of the cages in a zoo.

Most discussions, formal or otherwise, will be in the interests of, or at the request of, an individual or individuals. These people we can regard as being the 'meeting owners' and it should become their habit to make use of Exit Thinking. In Table 3.9 below is a simple checklist that each meeting owner should mentally complete before each social thinking discussion and mentally keep update throughout.

In making use of this, I cannot emphasize enough the importance of attention being given to the time available and the exit point of the discussion. At the end of the meeting the guillotine comes down and the participants leave the room. Another meeting might well follow at some point in time. But the subsequent meeting will need its own purpose and its own exit-objective. There will, in all practicality, be some different people involved, the flow of the discussion will be different and the energy will be different, and to regard the prospect of

Table 3.9 A simple checklist for leading meetings

To be completed by the meeting owner before each meeting

This is what we need to achieve by the end of this discussion ....

This is the job I would like you to do (to participants) ....

It will be my job to keeping focusing the discussion on the objective by ....

---

follow-up meetings as simply a continuation of a preceding meeting is a recipe for failing to deliver. It is one of the easiest 'get-outs' and another significant challenge to the rigor of Exit Thinking.

There are other methods that will keep social thinking on track. Importantly, these need to fit with the context to which they might be applied. If some of the techniques listed in Table 3.10 send a shudder down your spine or fill you with a sense of dread, don't worry; just keep reading on until you find approaches that do fit with your style.

Exit Thinking is very much a state of mind. Those who have diagnosed their Myers Briggs type and have found they have 'Sensing' and 'Judging' preferences will probably do many of the techniques in Table 3.10 without thinking and many more besides. Those who have different preferences may find it easier to follow the specific steps set out in this chapter. But whatever your natural style, Exit Thinking is about always keeping your eyes on the prize and about hearing the clock ticking on the time you have available. Forget time management, what we really need is time leadership – which brings me to my final thoughts.

The real job of leadership

The senior people that inhabit our organizations across the world have odd lives and stranger jobs. By comparison, it is easy to see what your local doctor or taxi driver does. It is easy to imagine what might be written on the job description of the chef, or the person paying out welfare benefits, or the scientist searching for a vaccine to combat disease. But our leaders; what exactly do they do? They seem fantastically busy. So much so that they need one, two, or sometimes a team of staff to support them – planning their every waking moment. They are well paid too so they *must* be doing something of immense value. They seem to travel around a lot. One moment in the head office the next on a plane to New York, London, Singapore, or Delhi. They hold grand titles showing their belonging this institute or that club. They look serious, very serious. But what exactly do they do?

The answer of course is that they talk. They hold conversations; they have breakfast meetings; they give presentations; they articulate the vision for the company; they chair formal gatherings. But above all they talk. Talk is the single most common activity in which senior people engage and it is the greatest tool in their toolkit. The doctor has her stethoscope or scalpel; the taxi driver his car; the chef has his kitchen; the welfare benefits administrator has her knowledge of

Table 3.10 Pick list of twelve techniques to keep thinking on track

1. State the ground rules (or protocols) at the outset of each meeting
   Some examples; all conversation will be on-topic, thinking will focus on solutions rather than problems, we will give our support to the chair to keep the discussion on target, we will make the best use possible of limited time together etc.

2. Follow an outcome agenda (and not a issue agenda)
   Some examples; agenda item – to leave the room with absolute clarity about the way forward, agenda item – to generate and agree at least three solutions to the problems of weak staff management, agenda item – to produce a draft announcement relating to the change of direction for the organization etc.

3. Deliberately compress the time available (nothing focuses the mind better). Do this knowing that it will catalyze thinking but that the results may need to be revisited for mistakes or missing issues

4. Use the 'parking lot' principle, for examples using a flipchart, to enable you to register, but not go into issues that are beyond the scope of the discussion

5. Use a skilled and independent facilitator

6. Require those present to produce something tangible by the time the meeting is adjourned
   Some examples; produce a draft communication statement, draw up the new structure for the organization, produce some guidance, produce a project plan etc.

7. Provide a visual reminder of the meeting purpose and pathway for getting there
   Some examples; a simple schematic visually showing what questions need to be answered (like stepping stones) in order to resolve the central-pupose of the meeting, a flipchart representing graphically what needs to be done in the meeting, in larger gatherings a poster on the wall articulating the purpose etc.

8. Have a large clock/timer strategically placed and visible to all in the meeting

9. Provide coffees at the conclusion to, rather than at the start of, the meeting

10. Hold stand-up 'bird table' meetings instead of fully seated meetings

11. Introduce 'lock-in' meetings where participants are required to remain with the meeting until the purpose is achieved (easiest for more senior people to call meetings of this type)

12. Spend time at the beginning of every thinking conversation talking participants through the importance of the topic and the how they can make a difference

intricate eligibility requirements; the scientist has her research lab, formulas, and test tubes. But the leader has only their skill in engaging others in meaningful conversation. Leadership takes place in that moment of interaction whether directly experienced or passed on in organizational stories or as staff vocalize their sense-making of what the leaders desire.

The problem is that there is a battle over leadership in each and every conversation and not perhaps the one you imagine. The battle is between the unseen habits, norms, and patterns of social thinking and the intention that any individual person might bring to the discussion. The job of inspiring people or bringing vision to others is tough enough, but to do so without an appreciation of the 'wiring beneath the board' of social interaction is madness. If talk is the job of leadership then leaders have to exercise mastery over the process of social thinking. Senior people, or for that matter anyone who leads thinking, should see the package of proposals outlined in this book as an expanded toolkit. And as we put some of the methods articulated in this book in context, for example, of organizational change, we can see that thinking channels, if selected appropriately, hold the key to more effective buy-in, to raising commitment and energy, to generating breakthrough ideas, and to delivering higher organizational performance.

Furthermore, whatever technical skills leaders had in their earlier years, these inevitably must fall away so that they can be replaced by skills and knowledge more relevant to the task, such as organizational design, horizon-scanning, and shaping organizational culture, to name a few. But all of these topics are preceded and followed by discussion with others. Theory or thinking about organizational design means nothing until people come together to collectively make sense of it. The introduction of 'integrated project teams' to replace 'functional silos' in and of itself means nothing. It only becomes meaningful through the implicit and explicit sharing of notions of what integrated project teams are. The announcement of an 'account management' structure within the organization hangs forever in the air like a giant air balloon until people grab hold of the rope, and through discussion, pull it back down to earth. It is through conversation and the exchange of talk that senior people can drive thinking forward about organizational design or whatever crosses their radar. This book offers part of the new skills set that leaders require.

But the beauty of it all is that the methods offered in this book can be mastered by all of us. We are asked to recognize that talk is important, to acknowledge that discussions drop into unseen channels of thinking, and to take responsibility for driving those discussions into much more profitable avenues. It really is as simple as that. The detail lies in the purposeful selection of words that trigger thinking channels and a broader appreciation of the need to manage the flow of energy and the road through to the exit or turn-off of any thinking conversation. This is a strategy that can be adopted by leaders, facilitators, change agents, chairs, and decision-shapers at any level. Could this be you? I am guessing that the answer is yes! So what more do you need to hear? It's important. It's important to you. It's easily introduced into your daily routine and it will instantly make a difference.

Notes

1 Thinking on Autopilot

1. Freesearch dictionary definition.
2. Google search engine.
3. Reduced by 25 per cent to reflect dual use of word 'fair' in reference to conferences, fetes, celebratory gatherings, markets, fayres.
4. Excluding the words 'investment', 'shares', 'capital', 'property', 'funds', 'mortgage', and 'money'.
5. A children's card game using picture cards. The aim is to slowly place cards face up on two different piles. When two face pictures match, the player to shout 'Snap' first wins.

2 Switching Controls to Manual

1. The Chatham House Rule originated at Chatham House in London in 1927 with the aim of providing anonymity to speakers and to encourage openness and the sharing of information. It is now used throughout the world as an aid to free discussion. It states that "WHEN A MEETING, OR PART THEREOF, IS HELD UNDER THE CHATHAM HOUSE RULE, PARTICIPANTS ARE FREE TO USE THE INFORMATION RECEIVED, BUT NEITHER THE IDENTITY NOR THE AFFILIATION OF THE SPEAKER(S), NOR THAT OF ANY OTHER PARTICIPANT, MAY BE REVEALED".
2. Action learning, as defined by North Eastern Illinois University is 'a continuous process of learning and reflection with the intention of getting something done. Learning is centered on the need to find a solution to a real problem. Learning is voluntary and learner driven, while individual development is as important as finding the solution to the problem.

References

10 DOWNING STREET (2005) http://www.number-10.gov.uk/output/Page7858.asp

4 MOONS BLOG MEDITATION (2005) http://4moons.blogspot.com/2005/05/meditation-is-hard.html

ASSOCIATION FOR RATIONAL THOUGHT (2006) http://www.cincinnatiskeptics.org/about.html

BERGER, P & LUCKMANN, T (1966) *The Social Construction of Reality: A Treatise in the Sociology of Knowledge* (Garden City, New York: Anchor Books).

CNN.COM (2 January 2000) http://transcripts.cnn.com/TRANSCRIPTS/0001/02/se.35.html

DEWEY, J (1991) *How We Think* (New York: Prometheus Books).

DYMER, C 'The Idea Loft' (2006) http://www.theidealoft.com/idealoft.html

GRAND HIGH LARRY, Mindfulness Meditation – Samatha (2004) http://www.erowid.org/experiences/exp.php?ID=24666

INTERNATIONAL ASSOCIATION OF FACILITATORS (2005) http://www.iaf-world.org/i4a/pages/index.cfm?pageid=3918

MCI WORLDCOM (1998) http://www.meetingsfare.com/real-costs.htm

NEW SCIENTIST.COM (18 March 2004) http://www.newscientist.com/article.ns?id=dn4797

SCHUTZ, A (1962) *Concept and Theory Formation in the Social Sciences from Collected Papers*, Volume 1 (The Hague: Martinus Nijhoff).

SHAKESPEARE, W (1984) *Macbeth*, 9th edn (London: Methuen).

STANFORD UNIVERSITY RATT (2006) http://www.stanford.edu/group/ratt/index.html

WUTHNOW, R (1987) *Cultural Analysis*, (London: Routledge).

Index